成长励志
系列

麦格希 中英双语阅读文库

影响世界的名人故事

Anecdote of Celebrities III

第3辑

[美]Milada Broukal ◎主编   吴淑珍◎译

吉林出版集团有限责任公司

图书在版编目（CIP）数据

影响世界的名人故事. 第 3 辑：英汉对照 /（美）布
鲁卡（Broukal,M.）主编；吴淑珍译. -- 长春：吉林
出版集团有限责任公司, 2012.7
（麦格希中英双语阅读文库）
ISBN 978-7-5463-9992-8

Ⅰ.①影… Ⅱ.①布… ②吴… Ⅲ.①英语－汉语－
对照读物 Ⅳ.①H319.4

中国版本图书馆 CIP 数据核字(2012)第 127633 号

影响世界的名人故事　第 3 辑

主　　编：（美）Milada Broukal
翻　　译：吴淑珍
插　　画：齐　航　　李延霞
责任编辑：沈丽娟　　孟广霞
封面设计：李立嗣
开　　本：650mm×960mm　　1/16
字　　数：220 千字
印　　张：10
版　　次：2013 年 1 月第 1 版
印　　次：2015 年 4 月第 3 次印刷

出　　版：吉林出版集团有限责任公司
发　　行：吉林出版集团外语教育有限公司
地　　址：长春市泰来街 1825 号
　　　　　邮编：130011
电　　话：总编办：0431-86012683
　　　　　发行部：0431-86012675　　0431-86012826(Fax)
网　　址：www.360hours.com
印　　刷：北京一鑫印务有限责任公司

ISBN 978-7-5463-9992-8　　定价：29.80 元

前言

英语思想家培根说过：阅读使人深刻。阅读的真正目的是获取信息，开拓视野和陶冶情操。从语言学习的角度来说，学习语言若没有大量阅读就如隔靴搔痒，因为阅读中的语言是最丰富、最灵活、最具表现力、最符合生活情景的，同时读物中的情节、故事引人入胜，进而能充分调动读者的阅读兴趣，培养读者的文学修养，至此，语言的学习水到渠成。

"麦格希中英双语阅读文库"在世界范围内选材，涉及科普、社会文化、文学名著、传奇故事、成长励志等多个系列，充分满足英语学习者课外阅读之所需，在阅读中学习英语、提高能力。

◎难度适中

本套图书充分照顾读者的英语学习阶段和水平，从读者的阅读兴趣出发，以难易适中的英语语言为立足点，选材精心、编排合理。

◎精品荟萃

本套图书注重经典阅读与实用阅读并举。既包含国内外脍炙人口、耳熟能详的美文，又包含科普、人文、故事、励志类等多学科的精彩文章。

◎功能实用

本套图书充分体现了双语阅读的功能和优势，充分考虑到读者课外阅读的方便，超出核心词表的词汇均出现在使其意义明显的语境之中，并标注释义。

鉴于编者水平有限，凡不周之处，谬误之处，皆欢迎批评教正。

我们真心地希望本套图书承载的文化知识和英语阅读的策略对提高读者的英语著作欣赏水平和英语运用能力有所裨益。

丛书编委会

Contents

Jonas Brothers

Mozart

01

Mother Teresa

Mother Teresa was a simple *nun*. She never wanted to be famous, but everyone in the world knew who she was. She received many important awards. She traveled around the world to accept them. She asked people for help. Then she gave everything to the poor.

Mother Teresa was born Agnes

修女特雷莎

修女特雷莎是一位普普通通的修女，她从来没有想过出名，但全世界的人都知道她。她得到过许多大奖，曾远行至世界上的不同地方来接受这些奖励。她请求人们伸出救援之手，然后，又将一切都施赠于穷人。

特雷莎于1910年生于现在叫马其顿的地方，她原名叫阿格尼丝·贡

---

nun *n.* 修女

Gonxha Bojaxhiu in 1910 in what is now Macedonia. She was the youngest of three children. Agnes's father died when she was a child. Her mother made dresses to support the family. Agnes's mother also liked to do charity work, such as visiting the sick. Agnes often went with her, and she enjoyed helping these people. She was a good and religious girl.

Even as a child, Agnes wanted to be a nun. When she was 18 years old, she joined a group of nuns in Darjeeling, India. There, she chose the name Teresa. Then she went to Calcutta to work at St. Mary's School. The school was in a *convent*. Sister Teresa lived in the convent and worked at the school for 20 years. She eventually became the principal. During all those years, Sister Teresa was always *concerned* about how other people lived. The convent had clean buildings and beautiful lawns. But outside the convent, the

克加·博亚久。她是她们家3个孩子中最小的一个。阿格尼丝很小的时候父亲便去世了，她母亲靠做衣服来维持家庭的生活。阿格尼丝的母亲也喜欢做善事，比如慰问病人，阿格尼丝常常跟母亲一起去，她乐于帮助这些人。她是一位善良的信教女孩。

甚至在儿童时代，阿格尼丝就想成为修女。18岁的时候，她加入到印度大吉岭修女团。在那里，她起名叫特雷莎。然后，她到加尔各答的圣玛丽学校工作，该校设在一座女修道院内。修女特雷莎住在修道院，在该校工作了20年。后来，她当上了院长。那些年里，修女特雷莎一直关心其他人过得如何。女修道院内有洁净的楼房和美丽的草坪，但是，女修道院的外面却是肮脏拥挤的街道，到处是穷困潦倒的人们。

convent n. 女修道院　　　　　　concerned adj. 关心的；忧虑的

streets were dirty and crowded and full of very poor people.

One day in 1946, Sister Teresa was riding on a train to Darjeeling. She looked out of the window and saw dirty children. They were wearing *rags* and sleeping in doorways. Sick and dying people were lying on *filthy* streets. She loved her work at the school, but she realized that other people needed her help more. At that moment, she believed God sent her a message. She decided to go to work with the poor.

Two years later, Sister Teresa left the convent. First, she went to a hospital to learn to take care of sick people. After three months, she was ready to live with the poor and the sick. One day, she saw a group of poor children and called them to her. She told them she was going to open a school. The school had no roof, no walls, and no chairs. On the first day, only five students came. She used a stick

---

1946年的一天，修女特雷莎坐火车去大吉岭。她向车窗外望去，看到一些很脏的孩子，他们穿着破衣烂衫，只能睡在过道上。她还看到有病及快要死的穷人躺在污秽的街道上。她热爱自己在学校里的工作，但她也意识到，其他人更需要她的帮助，需要她做得更多。在那个时刻，她认为上帝向她下了意旨，她决定去为穷人奔波。

两年以后，修女特雷莎离开了女修道院。她先到一所医院，学习如何护理病人。3个月之后，她作好了准备，要和穷人、病人生活在一起。一天，她看到一群穷孩子，便把他们叫到跟前。她告诉孩子们，她打算开办一所学校。实际上学校没有屋顶，没有墙，也没有椅子。第一天，只来了5个学生。她用的是一根棍子，在地上写字教课。

---

rag *n.* 破布；抹布　　　　filthy *adj.* 污秽的

to write lessons in the dirt.

Several months later, Sister Teresa had many students. Everyone in Calcutta knew about her. A friend let her use part of his house for the school. She taught the children language and math. She also taught them how to keep clean and stay healthy. Soon, other nuns came to help her. Sister Teresa was happy that they wanted to join her. But she told them that life with her was not easy. She said that everyone had to wear the same clothes—white cotton *saris*. She wanted all the nuns to look like the poor people in India.

In 1948, Sister Teresa started her own group of nuns. They were called the Missionaries of Charity. She was their leader, so they called her "Mother" Teresa. The nuns lived in the *slums* with people who were poor, dirty, and sick. It was hard work and the days were long. But many young nuns came from around the world to join Mother Teresa.

几个月之后，特雷莎有了许多学生，加尔各答的每个人都知道她了，一位朋友还让特雷莎使用他的房子的一部分当校舍。她教孩子们语言课和数学课，也教他们如何保持卫生和健康。不久，其他修女前来帮她的忙，她们愿意跟她一起干，这使修女特雷莎感到很高兴。但她告诉修女们，跟她一起生活不是件容易的事。她说，每个人都得穿同样的衣服——白棉布莎丽服。她想让所有的修女看起来都像印度的穷人。

1948年，修女特雷莎组建了自己的修女团。她们被称为"慈善传教士"。她是修女团的领导，所以，大家管她叫修女特雷莎"院长"。修女们和穷困、肮脏和病弱的人们一起住在贫民窟里，工作很艰苦，工作时间也很长。但是，世界各地许多年轻的修女都前来和修女特雷莎院长一起工作。

---

sari *n.* （印度妇女的）莎丽服　　　　　　　　　　　slum *n.* 贫民窟

One day, Mother Teresa saw an old woman in the street. She took her to a hospital. They refused to help the woman because she was poor. Mother Teresa decided to open a place for the sick and the dying. Later, she started homes for children without families. She also started clinics. Over the years, news of her work spread around the world. Many people sent her *donations* of money. Others came to work with her in India or other places. By 1990, the Missionaries of Charity were working in 400 centers around the world.

Over the years, Mother Teresa received many great awards, such as the Nobel Peace Prize. But she always said her greatest *reward* was helping people. Her message to the world was, "We can do no great things—only small things with great love." She died in 1997 at the age of 87. The whole world mourned her death.

一天，特雷莎院长在街上看到一位老太太，就把老太太送到一家医院。但医院拒绝给老太太治病，嫌她太穷。特雷莎院长决定为有病和濒临死亡的人开设一个收容所。后来，她还开办了孤儿院，创办了卫生所。几年当中，她的救济工作传遍全世界。许多人都给她捐款，有些人来到印度和她一起或在其他地方协助特雷莎工作。到1990年，慈善传教士组织在世界各地的400个中心开展工作。

这些年来，修女特雷莎院长获得过多次大奖，比如诺贝尔和平奖。但她总是说，她获得的最大回报就是能帮助他人。她向全世界传递的信条就是："我们做不了大事——我们做的是小事，但这需要有伟大的爱心。"特雷莎于1997年谢世，享年87岁。全世界为她的逝世而哀悼。

donation *n.* 捐款　　　　　reward *n.* 报酬

02

Sonja Henie

Sonja Henie was born in 1912 in Oslo, Norway. She started to ice skate when she was five years old. At age nine, Sonja won her first skating competition. Her family decided that Sonja should start to train seriously. Her father helped her, and she won her first national *championship*. Sonja was only 11 years old when she represented Norway in the Olympics in 1924. She finished in

索尼娅·赫尼

索尼娅·赫尼于1912年出生在挪威的奥斯陆。她5岁开始滑冰，9岁时赢得了她的第一场比赛。她的家人决定让索尼娅接受严格的训练。在父亲的帮助下，索尼娅获得了她个人的第一个全国冠军。1924年，她代表挪威参加冬奥会，年仅11岁。她滑了个最后一名，但她

---

championship *n.* 冠军地位；锦标赛

last place, but she got a lot of attention because she was so young. Sonja continued to train. She became a world champion and won a gold medal at the 1928 Olympics. She won two more gold medals in 1932 and 1936. Between 1917 and 1936, Sonja Henie won a total of 1,473 awards.

Henie had a very strong influence on women's *figure skating*. For example, she introduced music and *choreography* to skating. (Choreography is when you plan your dance to music.) She also introduced glamour to skating. Women skaters used to wear long, dark dresses. Henie wore beautiful, short, white costumes.

After she became a professional in 1936, Henie moved to Hollywood. She wanted to be a movie star! She appeared in several movies, and she skated in all of them. The movie company paid her $150,000 a year, which was a lot of money at that time. Sonja Henie

---

备受关注，因为她是那么的年轻。索尼娅坚持训练，终于在1928年冬奥会上成为世界冠军，赢得了一块金牌。在1932年和1936年她又相继获得两枚金牌。在1917年到1936年间，索尼娅总共获得了1473个奖项。

索尼娅·赫尼对女子花样滑冰产生了巨大的影响。比如说，她提倡将音乐和舞蹈技巧加入到滑冰中（舞蹈技巧就是按音乐编排舞蹈），她也将魅力融入到滑冰中。过去女滑冰运动员常常穿深色的长装，赫尼则穿着漂亮的白色短装。

1936年成为职业运动员之后，赫尼迁居好莱坞，她想成为一名电影明星！她曾在几部电影中出过镜，并且在每部电影里都是出现在滑冰的镜头中。电影公司每年付给她15万美元，这在当时是一笔不小的数目。索尼

---

figure skating 花样滑冰　　　　choreography *n.* 舞蹈设计

was a great success once again.

Everyone wanted to see Henie's movies because they were *glamorous* and *spectacular*. Henie skated in ice shows also. She went on a world tour with the ice shows, and the performances were always sold out. Her movie fans went to her ice shows and her skating fans went to her movies. When Henie appeared, there was always a crowd. Sonja Henie was a big star.

Henie was also a tough businesswoman. She made sure no one cheated her in her movie contracts or her ice shows. She loved money. At age 26, she was a millionaire. She became the richest athlete of her time. Henie married three times. All her husbands were

婭·赫尼又一次获得了巨大成功。

　　每个人都想看赫尼演的电影，因为这些电影既迷人又壮观。赫尼也在冰上表演节目中亮相。她开始在全世界作巡回冰上表演，每场表演的门票总是销售一空。她的影迷们争着去一睹她冰上表演的舞姿；而她的滑冰迷们则要争着去欣赏她在电影中的风采。只要赫尼一露面，他们就会蜂拥而至。索尼娅·赫尼成了大明星。

　　赫尼也是一名精明强干的经纪人，在她拍摄电影或滑冰表演签约时，她都要亲自落实，以免有人欺骗她。她喜欢金钱。26岁时，就已成为一名百万富翁了。她成那个时代最富有的运动员。赫尼结过3次婚，她的几任

glamorous *adj.* 迷人的　　　　　　　　spectacular *adj.* 壮观的

millionaires too.

Henie liked people to know that she was rich. She rode in a white Rolls Royce. She wore white dresses and a lot of jewelry. She lived in a mansion in Hollywood, and she had a *chauffeur*, a maid, a cook, a secretary, and a hairdresser. She gave big parties and invited all the most famous people to them. For one party, she put a tent over her tennis courts and hired people to fly to Hawaii just to get the best flowers. There were ice *carvings* everywhere and swans in the swimming pools. She always had the best food and drinks at her parties too.

Henie worked hard for her money. She worked very long hours.

丈夫也都是百万富翁。

　　赫尼喜欢炫耀她的富有。她乘坐一辆白色的劳斯莱斯车，她穿着白色的时装，浑身珠光宝气。她住在好莱坞的豪宅里，拥有一位司机、一位女仆、一位厨师、一位秘书和一位美发师。她举行盛大的聚会并邀请所有的社会名流参加。有一次聚会，她在网球场上搭建了一个帐篷，雇人飞到夏威夷，仅仅为了采购来最好的鲜花做装饰。那里到处都是冰雕，在游泳池里还有天鹅游憩。当然，在她的那些聚会上，她总是会提供最精美的食物和最高级的酒水。

　　为了钱，赫尼努力地工作着，工作时间很长。当她拍电影时，每天早

---

chauffeur *n.* （尤指富人或要人的）司机　　　　　carving *n.* 雕刻品

When she worked on a film, she got up at five o'clock in the morning, worked for 12 hours, came home, had dinner, and went to bed early. When she was on tour, she *stayed up* all night and slept half the day. Her diet was mainly raw eggs and *raw* beef. She wanted to have a healthy diet, but she ate very few vegetables.

In 1968, Henie and her third husband opened an art center outside of Oslo. This multimillion-dollar center contains most of her awards and her art collection, which is one of the best in the world. Fourteen months after the center opened, Sonja Henie died of cancer at the age of 57.

晨5点起床，工作12个小时，回家吃晚饭，然后很早睡觉。巡回演出时，她通宵达旦地工作，白天只睡半天。她的食物主要是生鸡蛋和生牛肉。她想拥有健康的饮食习惯，但她几乎不吃什么蔬菜。

1968年，赫尼和她的第三任丈夫在奥斯陆郊外开办了一个艺术中心。这个价值几百万美元的中心展示了她的大多数奖品和她的艺术收藏，是世界上最好的中心之一。中心开业14个月后，索尼娅·赫尼因患癌症去世，享年57岁。

---

stay up 熬夜

raw *adj.* 生的

03

I. M. Pei

I. M. Pei is one of the world's greatest *architects*. People admire his buildings in cities around the world. He is famous for his ability to combine old and new architecture.

Ieoh Ming Pei was born in 1917 in Canton, China. He was the oldest son of a wealthy banker. When

Ieoh Ming Pei

贝聿铭

贝聿铭是世界上最伟大的建筑设计师之一。人们非常赞赏他为世界各地城市设计的建筑，他以能够将新旧建筑艺术融汇在一起而闻名。

贝聿铭1917年生于中国广东，是一位富有的银行家的长子。9岁时，

---

architect *n.* 建筑师

he was nine years old, his family moved to Shanghai. At that time, Shanghai was a busy city with many new buildings. A 23-story *skyscraper* especially *fascinated* young Ieoh Ming. Over the years, he became more and more interested in architecture.

I. M. Pei received a good education at the best schools in Shanghai. His family lived very well and his childhood was happy. His mother was a talented musician, and Pei was very close to her. Unfortunately, she died when he was only 13 years old.

At that time, many wealthy Chinese families sent their children abroad to college. At the age of 17, Pei went to the United States. He studied engineering and architecture at the Massachusetts Institute of Technology (M.I.T.). He graduated in 1940 and wanted to return to China. But World War II had started, and Pei's father told him it was safer to stay in the United States. During the war, Pei worked for the United States government. His job was to find ways

---

他们家迁居上海。那时，上海是个繁华的城市，新兴建筑林立。一座23层的摩天大楼使年轻的聿铭特别着迷。年复一年，他对建筑越来越感兴趣。

贝聿铭在上海最好的学校里接受了良好的教育。他家境富裕，童年很幸福。他母亲是位很有天分的音乐家，聿铭与她很亲密。不幸的是，在他年仅13岁时，母亲就去世了。

那时，许多有钱的中国家庭都把孩子送到国外上大学。贝聿铭17岁时去了美国。他在麻省理工学院学习工程和建筑，1940年毕业后萌生了回国的打算。但是，第二次世界大战开始了，他父亲告诉他呆在美国更安全。在战争期间，贝聿铭为美国政府工作，研究课题是寻找安全地拆除建

---

skyscraper *n.* 摩天大楼

fascinate *v.* 使着迷

to safely destroy buildings. Pei did not like this work and was very happy when the war ended. After the war, Pei went to the Harvard Graduate School of Design.

Pei planned to return to China after he received his master's degree. But his father didn't agree. Again he could not go home. Pei stayed in the United States and worked for a building company in New York City. During this time, he designed homes, office buildings, parks, and shopping centers. Some of these buildings became famous.

In 1955, I. M. Pei started his own company. He designed many buildings for M.I.T. He also designed the Museum of Fine Arts in Boston. He became well known for creating buildings that looked like the things around them. This was very *unusual*. For example, for a building in the Rocky Mountains, he designed towers that looked

---

筑物的方法。他不喜欢这项工作，好在战争结束了，他很高兴。战后，贝聿铭去了哈佛设计研究生院。

贝聿铭打算在取得学位后回国。但他爸爸不同意，又一次他无法回到家乡。贝聿铭在美国为纽约市一家建筑公司工作。这期间，他设计了住宅、办公楼、公园和购物中心，其中有些建筑十分有名。

1955年，贝聿铭创建了自己的公司。他为麻省理工学院设计了许多建筑，还设计了波士顿的美术馆。他的创作以能使建筑与周围景物相映成趣而让人瞩目，这一点非同一般。比如，落基山中的一座建筑，他把塔楼群设计成看起来像山峦一般。

---

unusual *adj.* 不寻常的；与众不同的

like the mountains.

Pei was very successful. But one project almost *ruined* his career. In the early 1970s, his company designed the John Hancock Tower in Boston. The 60-story building was covered with blue-green glass. It looked like a huge mirror. Unfortunately, there was one problem— the windows started to fall out. Over and over, Pei's workers put in new windows. But over and over, they fell out again. Many newspapers in the country had stories about Pei's building. After a while, his company lost a lot of business. Eventually they discovered that the glass was not right. They replaced all of the windows and the problem was solved. Today, people think the John Hancock Tower is one of I. M. Pei's biggest successes.

During this time, Pei went abroad and designed buildings in Kuwait, Singapore, and Hong Kong. In 1974, he visited China for

---

　　贝聿铭一帆风顺，但是，有一个项目几乎毁了他的事业。在20世纪70年代初，他的公司设计了波士顿的约翰·汉考克大厦。这座60层的高楼上披着蓝绿色的玻璃墙，看起来像一面庞大的镜子。不幸的是，出现了一个问题——窗子开始往下掉。贝聿铭的工人们一次又一次地安上新窗子，但它们一次又一次地掉了下来。全国各地的报纸都刊登了这件事，为此，他的公司很快地失去了许多业务。他们终于发现，是玻璃不合规格。公司把所有的玻璃都换掉后，问题便解决了。如今，约翰·汉考克大厦被公认是贝聿铭的最大成功之一。

　　这期间，贝聿铭还去到国外，在科威特、新加坡和中国香港设计建

---

ruin　*v.*　毁灭

the first time in 40 years. He designed a hotel in Beijing. He also designed the 72-story Bank of China building in Hong Kong. This is one of the tallest buildings in Asia.

One of Pei's most famous works is the National Gallery of Art in Washington, D.C. It was a big *challenge* because he added a new part to an old building. His design was a big success. The president of France saw Pei's work and admired it. He chose Pei to design an addition to the Louvre museum in Paris. Pei added a glass and steel *pyramid* to the 700-year-old building. This was also unusual, because the Louvre is a traditional building and the pyramid is modern. At first, many Parisians were unhappy with the modern addition. But now, many people like his bold design.

I. M. Pei is someone who has truly influenced the modern world. He is a great success among architects.

筑。1974年，他40年来第一次访问了中国大陆。他在北京设计了一座酒店；还在香港设计了72层的中国银行大厦，这是亚洲最高的建筑物之一。

贝聿铭最著名的作品之一是华盛顿哥伦比亚特区的国家美术馆。这是一项极具挑战性的工程，因为他要在原先的旧建筑上续建新的部分。他的设计获得了巨大的成功。法国总统观看了贝聿铭的作品，赞不绝口。他选定贝聿铭为巴黎的罗浮宫博物馆设计一个附加部分。贝聿铭给这座具有700年历史的建筑添上了一座玻璃和钢结构的金字塔形附加馆。这是非同寻常的，因为罗浮宫是一座传统建筑，而这座金字塔形建筑的风格是现代的。起初，许多巴黎人对这个现代的附加馆感到不快。但现在，许多人都喜欢这个大胆的设计了。

贝聿铭是一位真正影响了现代世界的人物。他是建筑家中的佼佼者。

---

challenge *n.* 挑战   pyramid *n.* 金字塔

04

Eva Perón

Eva Perón was born in 1919 in a small village in Argentina. Her family was very poor. Eva always had big dreams. She wanted to be a famous actress. When she was 15 years old, she convinced a *tango* singer to take her to Buenos Aires, the capital city of Argentina. In Buenos Aires, Eva learned that big-city life was not

爱娃·庇隆

爱娃·庇隆1919年生于阿根廷的一个小村庄。虽然家境贫寒，爱娃却有着美好的梦想，她想成为著名演员。15岁时，她说服了一位探戈歌手将她带到了阿根廷的首都布宜诺斯艾利斯。在布宜诺斯艾利斯，爱娃意识到，大城市生活并不容易。她没有朋友、没有工作、没有工

tango *n.* 探戈舞曲

easy. She had no friends, no job, and no work experience. But she was determined to succeed. She got small parts in radio programs and began to make money. She became well known as an actress on the radio. Soon she was a *celebrity*.

Colonel Juan Perón was Vice President and Minister of War when he and Eva met. They immediately fell in love. He was 48 years old and she was 24. Juan Perón helped Eva get better jobs. Soon she became the head of all the radio stations in Argentina. Juan Perón became President in 1946. Eva worked hard for his *election*. She gave many speeches, and many people said she was one of the best speakers in Argentina. Five days after Perón's election, he and Eva got married.

As first lady of Argentina, Eva Perón worked very hard to help Perón's government. She became head of the Ministry of Labor and Health. Some people, especially those in the upper classes, did

---

作经验，但是，她决意要成功。她在广播节目中扮演了几个小角色，并开始赚钱。在广播里，她成了一位闻名的女演员，不久就成了名人。

当胡安·庇隆上校和爱娃相识时，位居副总统和国防部长，他们一见钟情。当时庇隆48岁，而爱娃24岁。胡安·庇隆帮助爱娃找了几份较好的工作。很快，她成了全阿根廷广播电台的总管。胡安·庇隆于1946年成为总统。为了庇隆的当选，爱娃付出了艰苦的努力。她发表了许多演说，不少人都称赞她是阿根廷最好的演说家之一。庇隆当选之后5天，他们结婚了。

作为阿根廷第一夫人，爱娃·庇隆工作非常努力，尽心帮助庇隆政府。她成为劳工与健康部的部长。有些人，尤其是那些上层人物，并不喜

---

celebrity *n.* 名人   election *n.* 选举

not like her. They thought that this ordinary actress had too much power. They *accused* her of spending too much government money on herself. Eva liked to look glamorous and wore very expensive clothes. One report said she wore 306 different dresses in 207 days!

Eva Perón decided that she wanted to help poor people. She wanted to change her image. She wore simpler clothes. She gave food, money, and clothing to the poor. Working people loved her and called her "Evita." She built houses and hospitals for the poor and the elderly. She also worked hard for women's rights. In 1947, her work helped Argentinian women get the right to vote. But she spent a lot of the government's money. People said she spent so much money that the government was *bankrupt*.

People were obsessed with Evita. Once when she gave a speech, nine people died in the rush to see her. When she visited Spain, 3 million people greeted her. In 1950, Evita started to look tired and

---

欢她，他们认为这个普通演员的权力太大了。他们指控她将大量公款挪为己用。爱娃喜欢打扮得妩媚动人和穿戴非常昂贵的衣饰，一篇报道称：她在207天中穿了306件不同的衣服!

爱娃下决心帮助穷人。她想要改变一下自己的形象，便穿着比较朴素的衣服，又将食物、钱和衣服送给穷人。劳动人民喜欢她，并管她叫"埃维塔"。她为穷人和老人建房子、修医院，她还努力争取妇女权益。在1947年，由于她的努力，阿根廷妇女获得了选举权。但是她花费了大量的公款。人们说，她花的钱太多了，以至于使政府破了产。

人们简直对埃维塔着了迷。一次，她演讲时，有9个人因争相一睹她的芳容而在拥挤中丧生。她访问西班牙时，受到300万人倾城出动的欢迎。1950年，埃维塔开始显得憔悴无力，并在公开场合晕倒过。医生发

---

accuse *v.* 控告　　　　　　　　　　　bankrupt *adj.* 破产的

she fainted in public. Doctors discovered that she had cancer. Her doctor told her not to work so much, but she didn't listen. She worked hard to get her husband re-elected, and in 1951 he won the presidential election for a second time. But Eva Perón's health was getting worse. She weighed only 70 pounds. When she appeared in public, she was so weak that her husband had to help her stand up.

Eva Perón died in 1952 at the age of 33. After her death, 40,000 people signed a letter to ask the Roman Catholic Church to make her a *saint*. For 16 days, people came from all over Argentina to mourn her death and see her body. So many people came that 120,000 people were injured in one day. All the flower shops in Buenos Aires were sold out.

Eva Perón's body was dressed and made up so she looked like she did when she was alive. Juan Perón wanted to make a *monument*

现她患了癌症，并劝告她别干那么多了。但她不听，她仍竭尽全力工作，以使她丈夫再次当选。1951年，胡安·庇隆第二次当选总统。但是，爱娃·庇隆的健康状况却越来越糟，体重只有70磅。当她出现在公众面前时，虚弱得必须由丈夫搀扶才能站着。

爱娃·庇隆于1952年逝世，年仅33岁。她去世后，有4万人签名致函罗马天主教堂，要求册封她为"圣徒"。16天中，阿根廷全国各地的人前来悼念她的逝世和瞻仰她的遗容。来人如此之多，仅一天之中就有12万人因拥挤而受伤，布宜诺斯艾利斯所有的花店全部告罄。

爱娃·庇隆以盛妆入殓，所以，看起来就像她活着时的装扮一样。胡

---

saint *n.* 圣徒　　　　　monument *n.* 纪念碑

for her. He thought that this would help him to be popular again. But he soon lost power and General Pedro Eugenio Aramburu became President. Aramburu wanted people to forget about Juan and Eva Perón. He didn't allow the monument to be built and wanted to get rid of Eva's body. There were many stories about what happened to Evita's body. After President Aramburu died in 1970, his lawyer gave the government information that solved the mystery. In 1971, *officials* opened the grave of a woman in Italy. They found the body of Eva Perón. The body had been there for 16 years. In 1976, the government buried Eva's body in her family's grave in Buenos Aires. No one will ever forget Evita, and today she is as famous as ever. Over the years, many people wrote books, songs, and plays about her life, including the famous musical play *Evita*. The legend of *Evita* will live forever.

安·庇隆想为爱娃立一座纪念碑,他认为这样会让自己再次受大众欢迎。但不久,他便失去了权力,佩德罗·欧亨尼奥·阿兰布鲁将军成为总统。阿兰布鲁想让人们忘掉胡安和爱娃·庇隆。他废止了纪念碑的建造并弄走爱娃的遗体。关于爱娃遗体的下落有许多传说。阿兰布鲁总统1970年逝世之后,他的律师向政府提供了揭开谜底的情报。1971年,政府官员在意大利打开了一位妇女的坟墓,他们找到了爱娃·庇隆的遗体。遗体已在那里安葬了16年。1976年,政府将爱娃的遗体葬于布宜诺斯艾利斯她自己家族的墓地中。谁也忘不了埃维塔,她今天依然和以往一样闻名。这些年来,许多人撰书、写歌和编剧来描述她的生活,其中包括著名的音乐剧《埃维塔》。埃维塔的传奇将永远流传。

---

official *n.* 政府官员

05

Stephen Hawking

There is a man driving around in a motorized wheelchair in Cambridge, England. He can only move his eyes and two fingers on his left hand. He *communicates* through a computer. He types words on the computer and the computer speaks for him. This man is Stephen Hawking. People know him for his courage and his sense of *humor*. He is also the greatest physicist since Albert Einstein.

Stephen Hawking was born in 1942 in Oxford, England. His father

---

史蒂芬·霍金

在英国的剑桥，有一位以电动轮椅代步的人。他只能活动眼睛和左手上的两个指头；他靠一台计算机与人交流，他把单词输入计算机，由计算机扬声器替他讲话。这个人就是史蒂芬·霍金。他的勇气和幽默感家喻户晓，他也是继阿尔伯特·爱因斯坦之后最伟大的物理学家。

史蒂芬·霍金1942年生于英国的牛津。他的父亲是一位研究热带病

---

communicate *v.* 交流   humor *n.* 幽默

was a specialist in *tropical* diseases. Stephen wanted to be a scientist too. He went to the University of Oxford and received a degree in physics. He then went to the University of Cambridge to study for a Ph.D. During this time doctors discovered that he had ALS, which is sometimes called Lou Gehrig's disease. This *fatal* disease weakens all of the body's muscles. Most people with ALS live for five years. The doctors thought Hawking would live for only two and a half more years. When Hawking heard this, he became very depressed.

At about this time he met Jane Wilde, a language student at Cambridge. They fell in love and got married in 1965. Hawking has often said that his wife gave him the courage to continue to study and work. Although Hawking had become more severely paralyzed, he became a professor at Cambridge. Luckily, the work of a physicist only requires one thing: the mind. Hawking had a son and then a daughter. He had another son 12 years later when his disease had

---

的专家。史蒂芬也想当科学家，他到牛津大学读书，并获得了物理学学位。其后，他去剑桥大学攻读博士学位。在这期间，医生们发现他得了肌萎缩性脊髓侧索硬化症(ALS)，有时也叫卢伽雷病。这种致命的疾病使全身的肌肉萎缩，大多数得了ALS的人只能活5年。医生们认为，霍金只能再活两年半。他听到这个消息后，变得非常沮丧。

大约就在这个时候，霍金遇到了简·怀尔德——剑桥的一名学语言的学生。他们相爱了，并于1965年结婚。霍金常说，他妻子给了他继续学习和工作的勇气。虽然霍金的瘫痪越来越严重，但他仍成了剑桥的教授。幸运的是，一位物理学家的工作只需要一种东西：头脑。霍金相继有了一儿一

---

tropical *adj.* 热带的   fatal *adj.* 致命的

gotten much worse. His youngest son has never heard his father's real voice. He has only heard the voice from the computer.

Hawking does research about how the universe began. He sees connections and works out explanations that other people cannot. His research has influenced many other scientists. Some of his ideas are so *advanced* that other scientists cannot prove them yet. His most famous ideas are about black holes. Black holes are not really holes. They are areas in space that are very dense. They are so *dense* that even light cannot pass through. That is why they are called black holes.

As his disease got worse, money became a problem for Stephen Hawking. He had a lot of medical expenses. He needed special wheelchairs, nurses 24 hours a day, and machines to help him read and speak. To earn extra money, Hawking gave speeches and published articles. Then someone told him to write a book that

女，12年后，当他的病情更加恶化时，他又有了一个儿子。他的小儿子从来没有听到过父亲真正的声音，他只能听到从计算机里送出的父亲的话语。

霍金从事宇宙起源的研究。他看到了宇宙中的联系，并作出了其他人作不出来的解释，他的研究影响了许多别的科学家。他的一些想法很超前，以至于其他科学家们还证明不了。霍金最著名的思想就是黑洞理论。黑洞并不是真正的洞，它们是宇宙中密度很大的区域，其密度大得连光都透不过去。这就是为什么称之为黑洞的原因。

由于他的病情越来越恶化，对于史蒂芬·霍金来说，钱便成了问题。他的医疗费用很高；他需要特制的轮椅、一天24小时的护理以及帮助他阅读和说话的机器。为了多挣钱，霍金发表演讲和出版文章。后来，有人建

advanced *adj.* 先进的；高级的   dense *adj.* 稠密的

explained the universe to ordinary people. Hawking agreed and wrote *A Brief History of Time*. The book sold over 8 million copies worldwide, and Hawking became a millionaire. Even though most people could not understand Hawking's ideas, he amazed them. Hawking became world famous. He met the Queen of England, he was on the covers of magazines, and he appeared on television shows.

In 1990, Hawking ended his 25-year marriage. This was shocking to many of his friends because his wife, Jane, was very devoted to him. She took care of all of his needs. She fed him, bathed him, dressed him, and raised their children by herself. Hawking left her for a younger woman—his nurse! They were married in 1995.

Hawking's strong personality and *spirit* have helped him to live with ALS for over 30 years. He has helped to make people aware of ALS and other disabilities. Hawking teaches us that even though a person is physically *disabled*, the mind has no limits.

议他写书，向普通人解释宇宙问题。霍金同意了，写出了《时间简史》。该书在全世界售出了800万册，于是，霍金成了百万富翁。尽管大多数人理解不了霍金的思想，但他让人们感到惊奇，因此霍金闻名全世界。他见到了英国女王，他成了杂志封面人物，他也出现在电视节目中。

1990年，霍金结束了他的25年的婚姻。这使许多朋友震惊，因为他的妻子简对他非常忠贞。简关照他的所有需要，给他喂饭，给他洗澡，帮他穿衣服，还自己带孩子。霍金离开她，是因为一位更年轻的女子——他的护士！两人于1995年结婚。

霍金坚强的个性和精神使得他能够与ALS抗争长达30多年。他帮助人们认识了ALS以及其他的一些残疾病症。霍金教会了我们：尽管一个人会在身体上患有残废，但心灵无极限。

---

spirit *n.* 精神　　　　　　　　　　　　disabled *adj.* 残疾的

06

Arthur Ashe

Arthur Ashe was one of the world's first African American tennis stars. He was a great athlete, and he won many *titles*. He became rich and famous, but these things never changed his good character. He never behaved badly. Ashe was fair, honest, and kind both in his life and on the tennis court. He also worked for many *charities* and always tried to help people.

亚瑟·阿什

亚瑟·阿什是最早的非洲裔美国网球球星之一。他是一位了不起的运动员，赢得了许多称号。他有了钱，出了名，但这一切没有改变他的高尚性格。他向来举止端正。无论在生活中也好，网球场上也罢，阿什一向公平、诚实和善良。他还做了许多善事，总是愿意帮助别人。

title *n.* 头衔；称号   charity *n.* 慈善

Arthur Ashe was born in 1943 in Richmond, Virginia. In that part of the United States at that time, African American people and white people didn't live, play, go to school, or even eat together. Arthur's father was in charge of the city's largest park for African Americans. Arthur played there every day. He was not good at most sports. But when he was seven years old, he played tennis for the first time. He liked it and played very well. His mother had died the year before, and Arthur played every day for hours to forget his sadness.

One day, a teacher at the park noticed Arthur's ability in tennis. He took Arthur to see a tennis teacher. Arthur learned a lot from him. Arthur became an excellent *amateur* tennis player. He won several titles. After high school, Arthur went to St. Louis, Missouri, to train with another *coach*. At the age of 19, he was one of the best young

亚瑟·阿什于1943年出生在弗吉尼亚州的里士满。那时，在美国的这块地方，非洲裔美国人和白人从来不在一起居住、玩耍和上学，甚至不在一起吃东西。亚瑟的父亲负责该城最大的非洲裔美国人公园，亚瑟每天都在那里玩耍。大多数体育活动他都不太擅长。然而，在7岁时，他头一次打了网球。他很喜欢网球，打得也很好。他母亲在他6岁时去世了，亚瑟每天都会打几个小时网球，以忘却悲痛。

一天，公园里的一位老师注意到亚瑟的网球技能，他带着亚瑟去见了一位网球老师，从那时起亚瑟学到了许多技术。他成了一位出色的业余网球手，还赢得了几个头衔。中学毕业后，亚瑟来到密苏里州的圣路易斯，

amateur *adj.* 业余的

coach *n.* 教练

players in the United States. Arthur won a scholarship to UCLA, the University of California in Los Angeles. He studied hard and graduated four years later. He also won many tennis tournaments and became the first African American man to play on the U.S. national team.

In 1969, Arthur Ashe became a professional. Six years later, he won the World Champion Tennis singles title and the Wimbledon singles title. He was the first African American man to win at Wimbledon and the first to be number one in the world. His success opened the way for African American players in tennis.

Ashe's great success did not come easily. Many times over the years he *suffered* because of *racism*. Sometimes, he was not allowed to play in tournaments. Other times when he played, people were

由另一位教练指导打球。19岁时，他就成了美国年轻的最佳网球运动员之一。亚瑟还获得了加州大学洛杉矶分校的奖学金，他学习很刻苦，4年以后毕业了。在许多网球联赛中他都获胜了，成为在美国国家队中打球的第一位非洲裔美国人。

1969年，亚瑟·阿什成了职业球员。6年以后，他夺得了冠军杯赛的网球单打世界冠军和温布尔登公开赛的单打冠军。他是温布尔登赛中获得决赛胜利以及荣膺世界头号选手的第一位非洲裔美国人。他的成功为非洲裔美国选手在网球界开辟了道路。

阿什的巨大成功来之不易。那些年里，他多次遭受到种族歧视。有

suffer *v.* 遭受　　　　　　　　　　racism *n.* 种族歧视

unkind to him. But Ashe was always calm and well mannered. He hated bad behavior on the court. He got angry only once, when his *opponent* said bad things about him because of his race. Still, Arthur didn't say anything. He just walked off the tennis court and did not finish the game.

Ashe met a photographer at a charity event to raise money for African American schools. Later they married and had a daughter. They named her Camera. Ashe was a devoted and loving father. He also taught his daughter to be a good and kind person. Every Christmas, he took her to give toys to children from poor families. Camera gave them some of her own toys too. Ashe had a lot of money, but he never liked to *show off*. At the end of his life, he owned only five suits and five pairs of shoes.

时，干脆就不让他参加联赛；有时，在比赛中，人们对他很不客气。但是，阿什总是保持冷静并且举止文雅，他憎恨球场上的无礼行为。只有一次，当他的对手以他的种族为由嘴里不干不净时，他生气了。不过，阿什仍然什么也没有说，他只是在比赛尚未结束时就激愤地走出了网球场。

　　在一次为非洲裔美国人的学校筹款的慈善活动中，阿什遇到了一位女摄影师。后来，他俩结婚了，有了一个女儿，他们为女儿起名叫卡梅拉。阿什是一位具有奉献精神和充满爱心的父亲，他也教育女儿要成为心地善良的人。每年圣诞节，他都带女儿去把玩具分给穷人家的孩子，卡梅拉也把自己的一些玩具分给他们。阿什已经很有钱了，但他从来不炫耀。在他临终时，他只有5套衣服和5双鞋。

---

opponent *n.* 对手　　　　　　　　　　　　　　show off 炫耀

Ashe was also very successful off the tennis court. He is the author of several books, including a complete history of African American *athletes* in the United States. In 1973, he received the Presidential Medal of Freedom, one of America's highest honors.

In 1979, Ashe had a heart attack. The following year, he retired from tennis. After that, he spent a lot of time helping young athletes and working for equal rights for all people. In 1983, he had heart surgery. Unfortunately, he got the *incurable* disease AIDS from blood he received in the hospital. Ashe continued to help people, even when he was very sick. Shortly before he died in 1993, he started an organization to help find a cure for AIDS.

阿什在网球场之外也很成功。他写了好几本书，包括一本记述美国的非洲裔美国运动员的体育史。1973年，他获得了总统自由奖章，这是美国的最高荣誉之一。

1979年，阿什犯了心脏病。随后的一年中，他从网球界退役。尔后，他花费大量时间帮助年轻运动员，并且为人们争取平等权利而努力。1983年，他做了心脏手术。不幸的是，在医院里从输入体内的血液中，他感染上不治之症艾滋病。即使在病中，阿什仍继续帮助他人。在1993年去世前不久，他还创立了一个组织，以帮助寻找治疗艾滋病的方法。

---

athlete *n.* 运动员   incurable *adj.* 不可治愈的

07

Diana Golden

Diana Golden grew up a happy, but *awkward* child in Lincoln, Massachusetts. She wasn't very good at sports. In fact, she was always the last person to be *picked* to be on a team. Sometimes she wasn't picked at all. But there was one sport

戴安娜·戈尔登

戴安娜·戈尔登在马萨诸塞州的林肯市度过了她幸福却不算出众的童年。她体育不太好。组队比赛时，她往往是同伴中最后一个被选上的队员。有时，同伴们根本就看不上她。但她特别擅长一种运

---

awkward *adj.* 笨拙的   pick *v.* 挑选

that Diana was very good at—skiing. Every weekend in the winter, Diana skied with her family. What she liked most was that she could do it by herself. She didn't have to wait to be chosen.

One day when Diana was 12 years old, one of her legs collapsed under her. She thought it was strange, but she tried to forget about it. Later, it happened again. Her parents took her to a doctor. Unfortunately, Diana had bone cancer, and her leg had to be *removed*. After her *surgery*, Diana was very brave in front of her parents and doctors. But when they left her hospital room she cried for hours. She kept thinking about how *miserable* her life was going to be.

Several days later, Diana asked one of her doctors if she could still ski. He said there was no reason why she couldn't. That made

动——滑雪。冬天的每个周末她都和家人一起去滑雪。她最乐意靠自己的能力去做事，而不必等别人来挑选她。

戴安娜12岁时，有一天她突然感到一条腿软弱不支。她感到奇怪，但试图把这件事抛在脑后。后来，这种情形又发生了。父母带她去看了医生。原来，戴安娜不幸患了骨癌，病腿必须被截掉。手术后，她在父母和医生面前表现得很坚强。父母和医生离开病房后，戴安娜却哭了好几个小时。她总是在想，未来的生活将会是多么凄惨。

几天后，戴安娜问医生她是否还能滑雪。医生说她没有理由不能滑

remove *v.* 移除；切除 　　　　　　　　surgery *n.* 外科手术
miserable *adj.* 悲惨的；痛苦的

her feel much better. While she was at the hospital, Diana saw other children die from cancer. She began to realize that she was lucky to be alive.

A few months later, Diana was ready to try skiing again. She was unsure of her abilities and she was afraid to fail. Her parents took her to a ski area that had a program called National Handicapped Sports. She saw other *disabled* athletes and she also met her ski *instructor*. He was a Vietnam war *veteran* with one leg, but he skied like a champion. He gave Diana the confidence and encouragement to make her dream come true.

With hard work and *determination*, Diana started skiing again. It was amazing. Soon she was skiing as well as she had before. One day during her junior year of high school, the school skiing coach

---

雪，这使她感觉好多了。住院时，戴安娜看到别的孩子死于癌症。她开始认识到她能活下来已算幸运。

几个月后，戴安娜准备试着再去滑雪。她对自己的能力没有把握，担心会失败。父母把她带到一块滑雪场地，在那里一个叫做"国家残疾人运动"的项目正在进行。她看到了其他残疾运动员，还遇到了她的滑雪教练。教练是个只有一条腿的老兵，但滑起雪来技艺高超。他给了戴安娜信心并鼓励她去实现自己的梦想。

戴安娜下定决心苦练，又开始滑雪了。令人惊喜的是，她很快就滑得和以前一样棒了。在她读初中时，一天学校的滑雪教练看到她在练习，

---

disabled *adj.* 有残疾的
veteran *n.* 老兵；老手

instructor *n.* 教员；教练
determination *n.* 决心

saw her practicing. He asked her to work out with the ski team. She started to train to make her body stronger, especially her leg, back, and arms. A year later, she competed in the World Games for Disabled Athletes in Norway. That same year, she won the *downhill* event in the World Handicapped Championships. Diana was filled with *enthusiasm*. She thought of nothing else but skiing, racing, and winning. Eventually Diana became the star of the United States Disabled Ski Team. Newspapers and magazines published articles about her. They called her a champion and a hero. But Diana didn't believe she was a hero. She was just doing her best.

After high school, Diana went to Dartmouth College. She trained with the ski team there in the school *stadium*. She had to use *crutches* to help her, but she ran and hopped up the stadium steps. There was

---

就让她和滑雪队员们一起练。就这样，她开始了正规训练，要让身体更强壮，尤其注意锻炼腿、背和臂膀。一年后，她参加了在挪威举行的世界残疾人运动会。同年，她在世界残疾人锦标赛中取得了滑降比赛的冠军。她满怀热情，什么也不想，一心只想着滑雪、比赛和取胜。戴安娜终于成了美国残疾人滑雪队中的明星。报刊纷纷登载有关她的文章，称她为冠军和英雄。但戴安娜不认为自己是个英雄，认为自己只是尽力做得最好而已。

中学毕业后，戴安娜进了达特茅斯大学。她和滑雪队一起在学校体育场训练。尽管她不得不靠拐杖协助，但仍在体育场的台阶上又跑又跳。戴

---

downhill n. （滑雪）速降
stadium n. 体育场

enthusiasm n. 热情
crutch n. 拐杖

a baseball field near the stadium where Diana worked out. Another student named Steve Brosnihan noticed her while he practiced. He admired her and liked her from a distance. But she didn't notice him.

During her second year at Dartmouth, Diana *quit* skiing. She felt *confused* about her future. She didn't know who she was or what she wanted to do with her life. She began to search for meaning in her life. She joined a religious group. She studied and read. But after a while, she realized how much she missed skiing.

After she graduated in 1984, Diana returned to skiing. She worked harder than ever to *build up* her strength again. She trained with both disabled and non-disabled skiers. With great determination, she began to build the greatest *career* in the history of disabled sports. In all, Diana Golden won 29 gold medals in world and national championships, including an Olympic gold medal in

---

安娜练习的体育场附近有个棒球场，有一个叫史蒂夫·布罗斯尼汉的学生在练球时从远处注意到戴安娜，对她产生了爱慕之情。但戴安娜没有留意他。

在达特茅斯大学的第二年，她放弃了滑雪。她对未来感到困惑，不知道自己会是个什么样的人，如何去面对自己的生活。为此她开始探索生活的意义。她参加了一个宗教团体，不停地学习、读书。不久，她意识到她仍然是那么想去滑雪。

1984年大学毕业后，戴安娜重返滑雪运动。她比以前任何时候都更加苦练，以重新增强自己的体力。她既和残疾滑雪运动员，也和非残疾的滑雪运动员一起训练。她抱着很大的决心，开始创建残疾人运动史上最伟大的事业。戴安娜·戈尔登总共荣获29枚国际和国家锦标赛的金牌，包

---

quit *v.* 停止；放弃
build up 增进；加强

confused *adj.* 困惑的
career *n.* 职业

1988. Throughout the 1980s, she continued to win medals and *awards* in both disabled and regular events. In 1988, she was named U.S. Alpine Skier of the Year. The U.S. Olympic Committee named her Female Skier of the Year. In 1991, she received the *prestigious* Flo Hyman Award presented by the Women's Sports Foundation.

Diana was on top of the world. She had a wonderful personality, a bright smile, and high spirits. She was smart and funny. Over the years, she did a lot for the disabled athletes movement. Because of her efforts and *triumphs*, people began to see disabled athletes as true athletes first, not just as disabled people. Diana was an *inspiration* to many people. She shared her feelings and experiences in articles, television talk shows, and speeches she gave around the country. She told people that they can have their dreams and overcome any problems.

括一枚1988年的奥林匹克金牌。整个20世纪80年代，她不断在残疾人和健全人赛事中获得奖牌和奖品。1988年她被授予美国年度高山滑雪优秀运动员称号；美国奥林匹克委员会授予她年度优秀女子滑雪运动员称号。1991年她收到了由妇女体育基金会颁发的享有盛名的弗洛·海曼奖。

戴安娜功成名就，非常幸福。她有非凡的个性、灿烂的微笑和顽强的意志，既聪明又风趣。多年来，她为残疾人运动做了大量的工作。由于她的努力和取得的成功，人们终于开始把残疾运动员作为真正的运动员看待，而不是只把他们当成残疾人。戴安娜开启了许多人的心灵。她发表文章，在电视上做脱口秀，到全国各地演讲，与人们分享她的感受和体验。她告诉人们，他们可以有自己的梦想并能战胜任何困难。

---

award *n.* 奖品
triumph *n.* 胜利；成功

prestigious *adj.* 有名望的
inspiration *n.* 灵感

In 1991, at age 27, Diana retired from competitive skiing. She continued other challenges. She liked to go hiking and rock climbing in the hot desert. Her life was calm for a while, but she soon got terrible news. In 1992, the doctors told her she had *breast* cancer. She had to have both breasts removed. She was brave in front of others, just like when she was a child. But inside she was afraid and angry. Several months later, there was more bad news. Her cancer had spread and she needed more surgery and more treatments. Diana became very *depressed*. One night, she took an *overdose* of pills. But she realized she had made a mistake and she called a friend. Her friend rushed her to the hospital, and thankfully, she survived.

After her suicide attempt, Diana searched for reasons to live. She got a *puppy* but a month later it died. One day, she got in her car and

---

1991年，戴安娜27岁时从竞技滑雪队退役。她继续向其他项目挑战。她喜欢在炎热的沙漠中徒步旅行和攀岩。她的生活平静了一段时间，但很快她又得到了可怕的消息。1992年，医生说她患了乳腺癌，并且必须切除两个乳房。像小时候一样，她在别人面前表现得很勇敢，但她内心既害怕又气恼。几个月以后，传来了更糟的消息，她的癌症扩散了，需要再做手术和进一步的治疗。戴安娜非常沮丧。一天夜里，她服了过量的药。但她意识到自己犯了个错误，于是便给她的一个朋友打电话。她的朋友赶紧把她送到了医院。谢天谢地，她活过来了。

作过自杀的尝试后，戴安娜寻找着活下去的理由。她养了一只小狗，但一个月后小狗就死了。一天，她钻进车里，向大山里驶去。她打算跳到

---

breast *n.* 乳房；胸部
overdose *n.* 药量过多

depressed *adj.* 沮丧的
puppy *n.* 小狗；幼犬

headed for the mountains. She was going to jump into a deep river. But once again, her will to live was too strong. She turned back and went to see a counselor. She got another puppy and named him "Midnight Sun" because he was her "light in the night."

Diana tried to make the best of things, even though it was sometimes difficult. She had a lot of friends, and she liked to go out and have fun. One night she met a man at a Halloween costume party. He was Steve Brosnihan, the student who had watched her train at Dartmouth. It seemed as if fate had brought them together again. On Valentine's Day while Diana was at the hospital getting her cancer *treatment*, Steve asked her to marry him. By then, the doctors had told Diana that she had one to five years to live. Steve and Diana got married in August 1999 and said in front of everyone there that they would love each other forever. They have learned to make the best of every moment they have together.

山谷中的一条深河中。但是又一次,她强烈的生存欲望促使她转头回家。她去看了一位心理医生。她又养了一只小狗,取名为"午夜的太阳",因为这只狗是她的"黑夜明灯"。

　　戴安娜尽力做好每件事,即使有时是很困难的。她有很多朋友,她喜欢外出游玩。一天晚上,她在万圣节前夕的化装舞会上遇见了一个人。他就是在达特茅斯大学看过她训练的那个学生——史蒂夫·布罗斯尼汉。似乎是命运又一次把他们带到一起。情人节那天,戴安娜在医院接受癌症治疗,史蒂夫向她求婚。那时,医生已告诉戴安娜,她只能再活1年到5年。史蒂夫和戴安娜于1999年8月结婚,在众人面前他们许下心愿要相爱到永远。他们已经学会了如何尽情地享受相依相守的每时每刻。

---

treatment *n.* 治疗

08

Tsai Erh-Ping
An Artist of Life

The vibrant colors of the *lizard* catch your eye as it seems to wiggle and crawl on the lady's sweater. Startled, you look closer and discover that you aren't looking at a real lizard at all. You're looking at a fanciful *brooch* made of ceramic, wire and precious stones. You have just been introduced to one of the fanciful creations of Tsai Erh-

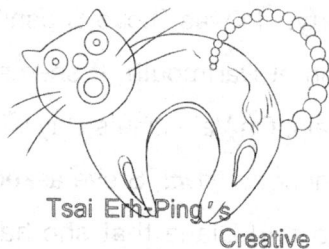

Tsai Erh-Ping's
Creative

生活艺术家——蔡尔平

只色彩鲜艳的蜥蜴非常抢眼，看起来好像是在一位女士的羊毛衫上蠕动爬行。大吃一惊的你，于是更靠近地看，这才赫然发现，原来你看到的根本不是真的蜥蜴，而是用陶瓷、铁线和宝石制成的创意独具的胸针。你刚才已经见识到蔡尔平充满想象力的创作，这位杰出的

---

lizard *n.* 蜥蜴

brooch *n.* 胸针

Ping（蔡尔平）, a remarkable artist who draws his inspiration from creatures of nature.

Childhood influences

Insects and lizards like this excited Tsai Erh-Ping's imagination in his youth and continue to excite him today. As a child growing up in the 1950s in rural Beigang（北港）in southern Taiwan, Tsai played in the fields surrounding his home. He chased *geckos* and decorated them with stripes or dots of paint.

His father, a medical doctor and artist in his own right, influenced his son a great deal. In fact, one of his father's *quotes* has become Tsai's theme in life: "Live in nature, live on nature, live for nature." And that is exactly what Tsai does.

艺术家喜欢从大自然的生物汲取创作灵感。

这类蜥蜴和昆虫从小就激发了蔡尔平的想象力，而且影响持续至今都不曾消减。他的童年时期是在20世纪50年代度过，在南台湾北港乡下长大的他，会在住家四周的田野间玩耍，还喜欢追着壁虎跑，还有在壁虎身上涂着条纹状或点状的颜料。

他的父亲是医生，本身也靠自学成为艺术家，他对儿子的影响非常大。事实上，爸爸的一句话成了蔡尔平一生的座右铭："生活于自然，靠自然而活，为自然而活"，而蔡尔平也奉行不渝。

年轻时的蔡尔平，进入国立艺专（译注：如今的国立台湾艺术大学）

---

gecko *n.* 壁虎   quote *n.* 引语；原话

As a young man, Tsai attended the National Taiwan College of Arts. There he met Cynthia Chuang, who became his wife and artistic partner. In his early 30s, Tsai moved with Chuang to New York. There they both studied at Parsons School of Design and received graduate degrees in *sculpture*.

Seeking to understand

Wanting to experience America, the couple traveled throughout the U.S., visiting national parks, major cities and museums . These experiences greatly impacted their artistic views. As these views developed, the couple became increasingly attracted to jewelry as a way to express themselves.

就读，并在学校认识了庄蕙芳，后来成为他的妻子兼艺术创作伙伴。他在三十出头时，和庄蕙芳一起到纽约，两人都在帕森斯设计学院进修，并取得雕塑硕士学位。

　　这对夫妻想深入体验美国，于是就在全美各地旅行，造访国家公园、各大城市和博物馆。这些经历对他们的艺术观点带来了莫大的影响。随着他们的艺术观不断发展，他们也开始愈来愈被珠宝所吸引，认为珠宝可以作为自我表达的一种途径。

　　对蔡尔平来说，从台湾和美国这两种他都生活过的文化背景中，思索着究竟该采用哪种文化的元素来融入作品中，其实并非易事。不过，后来

---

sculpture *n.* 雕塑

Contemplating what elements to select for his work from the two cultures he lived in was difficult. But gradually Tsai came to feel their meeting point was nature. Childhood memories of playing in the fields surfaced and sparked naturebased *creations*.

Always innovative, Tsai *refined* the traditional methods used to make ceramics so that he could create more intricate designs. In 1993, he won the Outstanding American Artist Award. In addition, Tsai and Chuang's jewelry has been shown at the Smithsonian in Washington, D.C., as well as many other museums.

他渐渐感觉到，这两种文化的交会点就是大自然。于是，童年在田间嬉戏的回忆就浮现脑海，并激起以大自然为主的创作灵感。

总是充满创新理念的蔡尔平，改良了传统陶瓷制作的技术，以便用来创作更精致的设计。1993年，他赢得了美国杰出艺术家奖。此外，蔡尔平和妻子庄蕙芳的珠宝，也曾在华府史密森尼博物馆和许多其他博物馆展出。

蔡尔平的创意并不限于珠宝而已，而是延伸到生活中的每个层面，其中也包括了户外。多年前，蔡尔平和妻子在纽约州长岛买下了一块不毛之

---

creation *n.* 创作　　　　　　　　　　　refine *v.* 改善；改良

Creativity at home

Tsai's creativity doesn't stop with jewelry but extends into every area of his life including the outdoors. Years ago, Tsai and Chuang purchased some barren land on Long Island, New York. There they built a home and *transformed* the land into a paradise. The trees, the shrubs, the flowers and even the rocks exhibit the creativity of these artists.

Reflecting their love for nature, the couple runs a kind of plant hospital in their house. Carefully examining plants and bushes cast aside in the surrounding area, Tsai and Chuang decide which ones can be saved. When given TLC, the plants flourish and are planted in the garden.

地，并在那儿建立家园，结果把那块地变成了天堂乐园，无论是树木、灌木丛、花卉，甚至是岩石，都十足展现出这两位艺术家的创意。

这对夫妻在家里简直像是开了一座植物医院，而这也正反映出他们对大自然的热爱。他们会仔细检查被丢弃在附近的植物和树丛，然后再挑选其中还能救活的，这些植物就这样在他们充满温柔关爱的呵护之下，逐渐恢复生机，成长茂盛，接着就会被植入庭园中。

蔡尔平在北港老家的后院，就是长岛庭园的灵感来源。他的家族在土地上栽种了数以千计的植物和树木，使得蔡尔平从小就很喜爱绿意，而且也很了解植物生态。后来他又回到北港家乡，并且重新装潢其中一栋住

---

transform *v.* 改变

Tsai's backyard in Beigang was the *inspiration* for this Long Island garden. His family *cultivated* thousands of plants and trees on their land, so since childhood, Tsai has loved and understood them. All of this came full circle when he returned to Beigang and redecorated one of his homes and created a tropical garden.

For Tsai Erh-Ping, who sees complex beauty in the littlest elements of nature, life is art – and art is life!

处，而且还打造了一座热带庭园，仿佛让一切又回归原点。

对蔡尔平这位能在大自然最微小的元素中窥见复杂之美的艺术家来说，生活就是艺术——而艺术也是生活！

---

inspiration *n.* 灵感　　　　　　　cultivate *v.* 耕作；种植

09

The World's Artist: Michelangelo

One look at Michelangelo's *masterpieces* reveals why he became a world-famous artist. During his lifetime, he mastered painting, writing poetry, designing buildings and making sculptures. Michelangelo was truly a one-of-a-kind artist.

His early years

When Michelangelo was born in Caprese, Italy, in 1475, his

艺术巨匠的养成：米开朗基罗

要望一眼米开朗基罗的傲世杰作，就不难了解他之所以会成为举世知名的艺术家的原因。米开朗基罗一生中，不但精通作画，还会写诗、设计建筑，也会制作雕塑，可说是真正独一无二的艺术家。

年少时光

米开朗基罗于1475年在意大利卡普雷塞诞生，当时母亲健康状况不

---

masterpiece *n.* 杰作

mother was in poor health. For that reason, he was sent to live with a stonecutter's family. There, the young child first learned to love cutting large pieces of stone into shapes.

Michelangelo later returned to live with his father in Florence. His father soon realized how intelligent the boy was and sent him away to school. Michelangelo, though, wasn't very interested in school and spent much more time drawing than studying. An art student that he knew *convinced* him to study the art of painting. But this angered his father, who wanted him to become a successful businessman or *merchant*. However, at 13 Michelangelo became an apprentice to a famous painter.

佳，也因为这个原因，他就被送到一位石匠家里寄养，小米开朗基罗就在那儿初次学会且热爱把大石块切割成不同的形状。

米开朗基罗后来返家在弗罗伦斯与父亲同住，而他父亲很快就发现这孩子的聪明才智，所以就把他送到学校去就读。只不过，米开朗基罗对学校课业不太感兴趣，花在画素描上的时间倒是远超过读书的时间。这时，米开朗基罗认识的一位学艺术的学生，劝服他去研修绘画的艺术，不料却惹恼了他父亲，因为他原本期望米开朗基罗能成为成功的实业家或商人。不过，米开朗基罗仍然在13岁时开始当一位著名画家的学徒。

---

convince *v.* 劝说；说服

merchant *n.* 商人

His famous works

Growing up during the Renaissance, Michelangelo was influenced by many great artists and works of art. Soon he was creating his own art, and by 16, he had finished his first two sculptures.

By 25, Michelangelo had completed what some call the world's greatest sculpture, the Pietà. The statue of Mary holding her dead son Jesus amazed everyone because of Mary's motionless *expression*. This was the only sculpture ever signed by the artist.

In 1501 Michelangelo began his next masterpiece, a *statue* of the

---

他的著名杰作

生长在文艺复兴时期的米开朗基罗，受到许多伟大艺术家和艺术杰作的影响，他很快就开始创作自己的艺术作品，而且在16岁时，就完成了生平头两件雕塑创作。

米开朗基罗在25岁时，完成了被誉为全球最伟大的雕塑：圣殇（译注：Pietà的意大利文原意是悲悯），这座圣母抱着耶稣遗体的雕塑，令众人大为惊奇，因为马利亚的表情很平静，而这也是唯一一座米开朗基罗亲自刻上自己名字的雕塑。

米开朗基罗在1501年开始制作下一个杰作，也就是圣经中的英雄戴

---

expression *n.* 表情

statue *n.* 雕像

Bible hero David. People *marveled* at the 5.17-meter statue because the human form was extremely lifelike.

Due to Michelangelo's fame, Pope Julius II selected him to paint the Sistine Chapel ceiling. Beginning in 1508, Michelangelo spent the next four years painting from a high, wooden platform. When he had finished, over 300 figures covered the chapel ceiling! Artists today still get inspiration from Michelangelo, the man many call the world's greatest artist.

维的雕像（译注：也就是少年时以石头击败巨人哥利亚的戴维王）。人们对这座5.17米高的雕像极为赞叹，因为戴维的身形极为栩栩如生。

　　米开朗基罗的名气如日中天，促使当时的教宗儒略二世选他来为西斯汀教堂的天花板作画。米开朗基罗在1508年开始作画，接下来的四年中都在木制的高台上作画。等一切终于大功告成时，教堂天花板上总共有超过300个人物。如今艺术家后进仍然持续受到米开朗基罗这位人称全球最伟大的艺术家所启发。

---

marvel *v.* 感到惊奇；大为赞叹

10

Davy Liu: Made for Making Art

Nearly losing his life before his first breath, Davy Liu began his remarkable story before his birth. While his mother was *pregnant* with him, the doctor checked and *detected* no heartbeat. Ten days later, just before a *surgery* to remove his body, the doctor doublechecked and found a heartbeat! Despite the near tragedy, Davy was born a healthy baby.

刘大伟：天生的艺术家

刘大伟可说是在诞生之前就已经展开了不凡的人生故事，因为他还没有呼吸到生平第一口气之前，就几乎葬送了小命。妈妈怀他的时候，医生在产检时检查不到心跳；但在10天之后，正当医护人员准备动手术摘除胎儿之前，医生进行重复确认，结果发现胎儿又有心跳了！虽然几乎酿成了悲剧，所幸刘大伟诞生时仍是一个健康的婴儿。

pregnant *adj.* 怀孕的；怀胎的
surgery *n.* 外科手术

detect *v.* 检测；探测

It appeared God had protected Liu's life for a special purpose. If so, it later became obvious that this purpose wasn't to make good grades. Liu struggled in school as repeated classroom failures discouraged him. But his father's interest in his drawings encouraged him, so Liu drew whenever he could.

Learning his love for art

At 13, his family immigrated to Florida from Taichung（台中）. Liu could *scarcely* communicate in English and *barely* kept up in school. *In addition*, being lonely made his first years in the States difficult. But he always looked forward to school art classes. Failing to shine in athletics or schoolwork, Liu felt his greatest chance of success lay in his artistic abilities. And these would soon make his greatest dreams come true.

这显示上帝似乎是为了某个特殊目的，而保守刘大伟的生命，而如果这是真的话，那么很明显这个目的并不是要他得到好成绩，因为刘大伟在学校读得相当吃力，课业上一再表现极差，令他相当沮丧。不过，父亲倒是对他画的图很有兴趣，使他备受鼓励，因此他总是把握时间来作画。

发现对艺术的热爱

13岁时，刘大伟全家从台中移民到美国佛罗里达州，当时他几乎无法用英语和人沟通，也很少赶上学校课业的进度。除此之外，寂寞的感觉也让他在美国度过的头一年非常难熬。不过，他总是很盼望上美术课，无法在运动项目或学校课业上发光发热的他，觉得自己最可能出人头地之处就在于他的各种艺术天分，而这些天分不久后果然使他美梦成真了。

---

scarcely *adv.* 几乎不

in addition 此外；而且

barely *adv.* 几乎不；几乎没有

Discovering his life's purpose

Liu realized early that he was born to create art. In eighth grade, he won a national art competition. And in spite of graduating from high school with a C *average*, Liu received a university scholarship to study art. He got his illustration degree from an art school, and The Walt Disney Company hired him, training him in *animation*. His first film *assignment* was designing sets for Beauty and the Beast – the first and only animated film ever nominated for a Best Picture Oscar.

Liu dreamed of Oscars while working on films like Aladdin and The Lion King. His national fame grew as he contributed to other

---

找到生命的目的

刘大伟很早就发现，他天生就是要来创作艺术。国二时（译注：美国学制的八年级相当于国中二年级），他在全美美术竞赛中脱颖而出；虽然高中毕业时，他的成绩总平均只拿到了C，却仍顺利拿到了大学奖学金，可以继续专攻艺术。他在一所艺术学校拿到插画的学位，而后迪斯尼公司雇用了他，并训练他绘制动画。他接到的第一个电影任务就是为《美女与野兽》设计布景，这部片是第一部、也是至今唯一一部被提名奥斯卡最佳影片的动画片。

刘大伟在从事电影《阿拉丁》、《狮子王》等电影时，原本梦想能拿到奥斯卡奖，而随着他为许多重要公司绘制插画，他在全美的知名度也逐

---

average *n.* 平均
assignment *n.* （分派的）任务

animation *n.* 动画制作；动画片

major companies. American Showcase magazine *dubbed* him the most unique illustrator in 1999, displaying his work on its cover.

Liu appeared to be achieving his dreams on the outside. Yet inside, he sensed he was missing out on a full life. He felt empty using his creativity to gain the *fickle* approval of people. By seeking higher dreams, he discovered deeper satisfaction in using his artistic creations to serve his Creator.

Kendu Films and The Giant Leaf

Liu began 2000 with a renewed sense of purpose and concentrated his efforts on bringing a new concept to the big screen. During the following four years, he worked on founding Kendu

---

渐窜升，并在1999年被《美国展示》杂志誉为风格最独特的插画家，同时封面选用他的作品。

不过，刘大伟虽然在外表上似乎已经达成梦想了，但是在内心深处，却感觉自己没能过个圆满的生活，对于运用自己的创造力来取得人们善变的认可，他也感到非常空虚。他于是改追求更崇高的梦想，发现利用自己的艺术创作来服侍造物主，反而能获得更大的满足。

康多影业和梦中的巨叶

刘大伟在2000年开始重新对生命有了使命感，并把全部精力投注于让一个新理念登上大银幕。接下来的四年中，他积极筹划成立康多影业，这家动画制作公司为包括皮克斯、迪斯尼、索尼和可口可乐等知名企业提

---

dub *v.* 授予……

fickle *adj.* 无常的；易变的

Films. This animation production company offers all kinds of artistic media services to bigname *clients* from Pixar and Disney to Sony and Coca-Cola. But the company is also constantly working on its own projects: children's books that will eventually become feature films.

Kendu Films aims to create stories that build character by telling Bible stories from animals' *perspectives*. *The Giant Leaf*, for example, tells of three animals that chase their dreams and accidentally discover their *salvation* from a flood. Those familiar with the story of Noah using a boat to save Earth's creatures from a global flood recognize the book's roots. With the success of this children's book, Kendu Films hopes to complete the movie version by 2012.

Liu is *convinced* he has discovered his life's purpose. So he produces admirable artwork and inspiring stories to lead others to discover their own reason for being.

供艺术媒体服务。不过，公司本身也持续致力于自己的计划：包括最终将改编成电影的童书系列。

康多影业计划创作出能陶冶品格的故事，并透过动物的观点来诉说圣经的故事。例如，《梦中的巨叶》就讲述三只追逐梦想的动物，最后意外获得拯救，免于被大洪水淹没；对诺亚的故事很熟悉的人，不难看出这本书的渊源，诺亚利用方舟来拯救地球上的动物，使人们不至于被全球性的大洪水所淹灭。由于这本童书广受欢迎，因此康多影业打算在2012年完成该书的电影版。

刘大伟确信，他已经找到了生命的目的，因此将持续推出令人赞赏的艺术杰作和鼓舞人心的故事，希望能引导其他人也能发现他们存在的目的。

---

client *n.* 客户；顾客
salvation *n.* 救助；拯救

perspective *n.* 观点；看法
convinced *adj.* 确信；深信

11

A Life of Dance

Chang Feng-Hsiang （张凤翔）lay awake. She was facing one of the hardest decisions she would ever have to make. She had come to Spain to study *flamenco* and follow her dream of becoming a world-class dancer. And now she had been offered a place in a professional dance company. Though staying in Spain was a *temptation*, it meant a long separation from her husband and children in Taiwan. Chang didn't know what to do.

Chang Feng-Hsiang

舞动人生

张凤翔辗转难眠，因为她正面临有生以来最困难的抉择。她为了研习弗朗明哥舞而来到西班牙，希望能圆一个想当世界级舞者的梦，而如今她已获得参与一个（西班牙）职业舞团的邀约。虽然留在西班牙发展的确是个很大的诱惑，但那代表必须和台湾的丈夫和孩子长期相隔两地。张凤翔真的不知该如何是好。

flamenco *n.* 弗朗明哥舞　　　　　　temptation *n.* 诱惑

A life of dance

Music and dance had always been important parts of Chang's life. Under the influence of her grandfather, a *composer* and folk artist, the entire family became involved in music, drama and dance. Her family supported itself by working as a performance *troupe*. At age 4, Little Rabbit — as Chang was called — began performing solo dances during her family's shows. By age 7, she was performing professionally.

In the 1950s, Taiwan was poor, so Chang's family moved around, performing on any stage they could find. With each performance, Little Rabbit's *celebrity* grew. By 15 she was appearing weekly on television.

Putting family first

After that sleepless night in Spain, Chang knew she had to return to her family. Doing so could have meant the end of her professional

---

舞蹈人生

音乐和舞蹈一直在张凤翔生命中占有很重要的地位。在作曲家兼民俗艺术家的爷爷的熏陶影响下，张家全家都投入到音乐、戏剧和舞蹈中，并组成表演团维生。4岁时，绰号小白兔的张凤翔就开始在张家的演出中表演独舞。等到7岁时，她已经开始职业表演了。

在1950年代，台湾仍是个贫穷的国度，因此张凤翔的家人必须四处迁移，以便在任何舞台上表演。随着每次的演出，小白兔的名气也愈来愈高。15岁时，她开始每周都出现在电视荧光幕上。

家人摆在第一

在西班牙度过的那个无法成眠的夜晚之后，张凤翔知道，她必须回到家人身边。虽然此举可能会葬送她的职业生涯，但令她大感意外的是，这

---

composer *n.* 作曲家
celebrity *n.* 名气；名声

troupe *n.* 演出团；歌舞团

life, but to her surprise, it was only the beginning. Back in Taiwan, she continued to perform on TV. At one point, she was able to go to Japan and continue studying dance — with her dance teacher from Spain.

But dance was becoming less important in her life. Her beloved family was growing, and in 1984 they immigrated to the United States. There, she lived with four generations of her family, eventually caring for her grandchildren. Though she continued to produce dance shows, it looked as though her dancing days were over.

But in 2007, while listening to her granddaughter play the piano, Chang started to dance again. Her family saw her dancing and encouraged her to return to Spain and continue with her training. Years before, Little Rabbit had chosen her family over her dreams. But now, with her family's *enthusiastic* support, she has returned to her dream of becoming a world-class dancer.

反而是她生涯起飞的开端。回到台湾之后,她继续在电视上演出。在某段时期,她还去到了日本,持续研习舞蹈——向她在西班牙的同一位舞蹈老师学习。

不过,舞蹈在她生命中的重要性却变低了。她心爱的家庭增添了生力军,到了1984年,全家移民美国。在那儿,她和家人四代同堂,最后还照顾起小孙子来。虽然她持续制作舞蹈秀,但她的舞蹈生涯看似已经划上了句点。

可是到了2007年,张凤翔听孙女弹钢琴的时候,又不禁开始舞动起来。她的家人看到了她的舞蹈,便鼓励她回到西班牙,继续舞蹈训练。多年前,小白兔曾选择了自己的家人,而放弃了自己的梦想。但如今,有了家人热情的支持,她又找回了那个想当世界级舞者的梦。

---

enthusiastic *adj.* 热情的;热心的

12

In William's Words

What's in a name?

Genius — if your name happens to be William Shakespeare. The name "William Shakespeare" is among the most recognized and *revered* in history. Widely known as a literary genius, the famed playwright and poet has *earned* such nicknames

William Shakespeare

as the *Bard* and England's national poet. His plays have been

用莎士比亚的话说

名字有什么意义呢？

（译注：出自莎士比亚剧作《罗密欧与朱丽叶》，朱丽叶说：What's in a name? That which we call a rose by any other name would smell as sweet. [玫瑰即使换了一个名字，也一样芬芳]）

答案是天才——如果你的名字刚好是莎士比亚的话。"威廉·莎士比亚"这个名字堪称史上最为人所知、也最受尊崇的大名之一。被广泛视为文学天才的这位著名剧作家兼诗人，还赢得了诗翁和英国国家诗人的封

---

revere *v.* 尊敬；崇敬
bard *n.* 诗人

earn *v.* 赢得

translated into every major language and are performed more often than those of any other playwright. Even today his creative achievements have yet to be *surpassed*. Still, in spite of his fame, very little is known about the man himself.

It is believed that William Shakespeare was born on April 23, 1564, in Stratford-on-Avon. As a boy, he likely attended grammar school and studied subjects like Greek and Latin literature. However, for reasons unknown, Shakespeare left school when he was 15 and never again *pursued* formal education. Just three years later, in 1582, he married Anne Hathaway, a woman eight years his senior. Soon after, they started a family.

号。他的剧作被翻译成全球各大主要语言，而且演出的场次远超出任何其他剧作家。甚至一直到今天他创意非凡的成就仍然无人能及（译注：直译为尚待后人超越），只不过，虽然莎翁名气如日中天，但有关他本人的身世却鲜为人知。

据信莎士比亚于1564年4月23日诞生于亚文河畔的斯特拉特福。他小时候可能有就读文法学校，并研习希腊和拉丁文学等课程。不过，他因为不明原因而在15岁中断学业，从此再也没接受过正规教育。仅仅3年之后，也就是1582年，他娶了安·海瑟维这位大他8岁的女子为妻。不久后，他们就拥有了自己的小家庭。

---

surpass v. 超过；超越   pursue v. 追求

No one really knows how or when Shakespeare first began writing and acting, but by the 1590s his interest in these areas had gained *momentum*. As a result, he left Stratford-on-Avon and moved to London to pursue his dreams.

All the world's a stage

Theater was the primary source of entertainment during the Elizabethan Era, and Queen Elizabeth herself was likely one of its biggest *patrons*. A *superb* talent like Shakespeare no doubt flourished in it. Aside from being a playwright, Shakespeare was also a well-known actor during his lifetime. And since actors of the day were *jacks-of-all-trades*, it can be assumed that Shakespeare was skilled

没有人知道莎士比亚究竟是如何或何时开始写作和演戏的，只知道在16世纪90年代时，他对上述领域的兴趣变得非常浓厚。结果他为此离开了亚文河畔的斯特拉特福，并搬到伦敦寻梦。

世界是舞台（译注：All the world's a stage出自莎士比亚剧作As You Like It "皆大欢喜"的贾克斯所言）

在伊丽莎白一世时代，戏剧是主要的娱乐来源，而伊丽莎白女王本身很可能就是最大的赞助人之一，而像莎士比亚这样超凡绝伦的天才，在当时的环境里自然容易大展才华。他除了是剧作家之外，在世时也是著名的演员，而由于当时演员往往必须多才多艺，因此可以推定莎士比亚同样也

momentum *n.* 冲力；势头
superb *adj.* 超凡的
patron *n.* 赞助人
jacks-of-all-trades *n.* 多才多艺

in dancing, singing, *acrobatics* and playing musical instruments. He rose to fame when he joined The Lord Chamberlain's Men, an acting company protected by the Queen herself.

And it wasn't just his acting that impressed the Queen. As a *prolific* writer, Shakespeare made quite a name for himself, even during his day. His plays were often *purchased* and performed for large audiences in locations such as the famous Globe Theatre, of which Shakespeare was part owner. Records show that The Lord Chamberlain's Men performed at least two of Shakespeare's plays before the Queen and her court, further affirming Shakespeare's

---

擅长舞蹈、歌唱、杂技和弹奏乐器。他加入侍从长剧团后开始名气大噪，而庇荫该剧团的正是女王本人。

莎士比亚令女王印象深刻的不只是他的演技，即使在当时，他身为多产作家的资历，也为自己赢得了不小的名声。他的剧作往往被买下，并于一些地点在众多观众面前演出，而演出的场地包括了著名的莎士比亚环球剧院，莎士比亚本人也是剧院所有人之一。记录显示，侍从长剧团曾在女王和王室人员座前演出过至少两出莎翁戏剧，这点更进一步证实了莎士比亚的名气和才气。即使在16世纪90年代疫病暴发期间（译注：黑死病）伦敦各地的剧院都纷纷关闭，但莎士比亚仍持续撰写剧作和诗作，它们终

---

acrobatic *n.* 杂技   prolific *adj.* 多产的；作品丰富的
purchase *v.* 买；购买

fame and talent. Even as the *plague* shut down theaters all over London in the 1590s, Shakespeare continued to pen plays and poetry that would eventually make history.

To be or not to be

Shakespeare is credited with authoring an impressive 37 plays and 154 sonnets and is widely remembered for his creative achievements. However, his works are not without *controversy*. Some people doubt that Shakespeare wrote the works credited to him and propose other people as the true authors. Theories *abound* supporting more educated individuals as the likely writers. Most people disagree with these claims, however, instead giving

---

将名留青史。

是还是不是呢？

（译注：To be or not to be为莎士比亚戏剧《哈姆雷特》中哈姆雷特王子的名言，有文学评论家指意思是"活好，还是自杀好"，但也有其他人引申为各种不同的意涵，例如："去做好，还是不做好"，此处则指"是莎士比亚写的，还是不是莎士比亚写的"）

莎士比亚被公认有37部剧作和154首十四行诗，令人印象深刻，并以创意非凡的成就令众人永难忘怀。不过，他的作品也并非没有争议性，因为有些人怀疑莎士比亚真的亲手写了那些作品，并提出其他可能是真正作者的人选，支持其他受过更高教育的人选才是可能的作者的推测，更是漫天飞。只不过，大多数人仍然不同意那些宣称，认为莎士比

---

plague *n.* 瘟疫
abound *v.* 大量存在；充满

controversy *n.* 争议；争论

Shakespeare credit where credit is due.

Words, words, words

Shakespeare's genius really shows when it comes to his vocabulary. Some experts claim that he knew over 29,000 words, thus making him a vocabulary genius! And when he couldn't come up with an *appropriate* word in his writing, he invented a new one. In fact, Shakespeare *coined* over 1,700 words commonly used in the English language today and popularized others that were already

---

亚实至名归。

文字、文字、文字

（译注：Words, words, words出自莎士比亚剧作《哈姆雷特》，大臣波洛涅斯询问哈姆雷特在阅读什么，哈姆雷特便作此回答）

莎士比亚在所使用的语汇上，真正展现了他的杰出天分。一些专家宣称，他熟知超过290,000字，因此堪称字汇天才！而且，每当他写作时想不出适合的字时，就会发明新字。事实上，莎士比亚创造了1700多个字（译注：此指经牛津英文字典的研究与查证，这些字最先出现在莎士比亚的作品中，而无法在更早的其他典籍中找到。例如，有些情况是，原本英文中已有某字，但莎士比亚加以其他字尾的变化而首创了新的用法），而

---

appropriate *adj.* 合适的；适当的　　　　coin *v.* 创造（新词语）

in use. Among words credited to him are amazement, *assassination*, downstairs, employer, fashionable, silliness and useful. Phrases and idioms include break the ice, come what may, and love is blind.

For Shakespeare, it seems all's well that ends well. As each play comes to the stage or screen again, his genius continues to live on through his words.

且它们一直到今天仍是常用的英文字，此外，他也让一些已经在使用中的字变得更流行起来。被认为要归功于莎士比亚的字包括了amazement（惊奇）、assassination（暗杀）、downstairs（楼下）、employer（雇主）、fashionable（时髦的）、silliness（愚蠢）以及useful（有用的）（译注：此选用了一些和今日意思相同的英文字，但由于时代的变迁，也有些字的意义已经和现在不同了）。短语和俗语包括break the ice(打破僵局)、come what may和love is blind（爱情是盲目的）

对莎士比亚来说，似乎只要结局圆满就皆大欢喜（译注：all's well that ends well [终成眷属] 也是莎翁名剧之一，作者在此玩文字游戏）。随着莎士比亚的剧作一再被搬演到舞台或大银幕上，他的傲世天才就会持续活在他笔下的文字中。

---

assassination *n.* 暗杀

13

Franz Joseph Haydn
Master Composer

Franz Joseph Haydn (1732-1809) had a long and prolific musical career, composing countless pieces of music over five *decades*. His significant contributions to *symphony* and string *quartet* music influenced musicians like his friend Mozart and student Beethoven and *ushered* in music's classical period.

交响乐之父：海登

法兰兹·约瑟夫·海登（1732－1809年）拥有漫长又多产的音乐生涯，在五十多年期间谱出了不计其数的曲子，而他对交响乐和弦乐四重奏的卓越贡献，则影响了包括他的朋友莫扎特和学生贝多芬等音乐家，开创音乐界古典时期的先河。

---

decade *n.* 十年

quartet *n.* 四重奏

symphony *n.* 交响曲

usher *v.* 开创；开启

From singing to writing music

Son of a music-loving wheel maker, Haydn was sent to a relative's for music training when he was only 6. Discovered by a *choir* director two years later, the young boy became a *treble* in the St. Stephen's Cathedral boys choir in Vienna, Austria.

When Haydn turned 17, his voice matured, and he could no longer sing the high notes, so he was subsequently dismissed from the choir. Staying in Vienna, he taught and performed music to make ends meet, all the while teaching himself music theory and composition. In 1761, the 29-year-old Haydn landed a job as Kapellmeister for the royal Esterházy family. His responsibilities *comprised* managing an *orchestra* and composing music for the prince. Haydn flourished in the steady employ of appreciative masters. He once said, "I could ... make experiments, observe what created

---

从歌唱到作曲

海登身为热爱音乐的轮胎匠之子，年仅6岁时就被送到亲戚家学习音乐。两年后，诗班主任发现了海登这个小男孩的天分，于是他加入了奥地利维也纳圣史蒂芬教堂少年诗班，担任高音部男童歌手。

等到海登17岁时，他的童音变嗓，再也唱不上高音，于是后来退出诗班。他待在维也纳的期间，靠教授和表演音乐勉强维持生计，在此同时，他也自修乐理和作曲。1761年，29岁的海登受聘担任艾斯特哈吉王室家族的乐长，职责包括管理管弦乐团及为亲王作曲。海登得以在欣赏他的大师旗下拥有稳定的工作，音乐长才愈发茁壮。他曾说过："我可以……进行实验，并注意到哪些元素会令人印象深刻，而哪些则会削弱印

---

choir *n.* 唱诗班

comprise *v.* 包括；由……组成

treble *n.* 男童高音

orchestra *n.* 管弦乐队

an impression, and what weakened it, thus improving, adding to, cutting away, and running risks."

Haydn's music

No single word can describe Haydn's music, which is at times upbeat, even playful, and at times serious and *meditative*. As Kapellmeister, Haydn composed music for twice-weekly concerts. These compositions ranged from *chamber music* to symphonies and operas. The remoteness of the Esterháza palace, where he spent much of his time, enabled him to be creative. Haydn said, "There was nobody in my *vicinity* to confuse and annoy me in my course, and so I had to become original."

Enduring fame

After 18 years with the Esterházys, Haydn's fame had grown

象，因而得以改进、增添、删减和勇于冒险。"

海登的音乐

海登的音乐难以一语道尽，他的音乐有时激昂乐观，甚或戏谑，时而却严肃又令人沉思。他担任乐长期间，会为每周两场音乐会创作音乐，作品从室内乐、交响乐，到歌剧都有。他多数时间都生活在地处偏僻的艾斯特哈吉宫，这反而使他创造力十足。海登曾说："在我住所附近，没有闲杂人等来混淆和干扰我的行事进度，所以我必定变得具有原创性。"

名气持久不坠

服务艾斯特哈吉家族18年后，海登的名声大增，亲王家族于是允许

---

meditative *adj.* 沉思的；深思的   chamber music 室内乐
vicinity *n.* 附近；近郊

so much that the family allowed him to write for others and sell his music. *Commissions* from abroad came pouring in. In 1790 he traveled to London and made a second trip in 1794. The English loved him *immensely*; one critic even said, "Like our own Shakespeare, [Haydn] moves and governs the passions at his will."

In the midst of Napoleon's conquest of Vienna in May 1809, Haydn, 77, lay on his deathbed. The French *conqueror* paid Haydn the final honor of stationing guards to protect the master composer's home from French troops. Today, Haydn is honored as the Father of the Symphony, and his music continues to entertain and inspire.

他为其他人谱曲和出售自己的音乐作品，来自海外委托作曲的案子于是源源而来。他在1790年造访伦敦，又在1794年二度造访。当时英国人立即对他非常爱戴，有位评论家甚至说："（海登）就像英国本国的莎士比亚一样，能随心所欲地感动和操控他人的热情。"

1809年5月，拿破仑占领维也纳期间，77岁的海登已濒临死亡边缘，而这位法国侵略者对海登致上最后敬意，派驻守卫站岗，保护这位作曲大师的家园，使不受法军干扰。如今海登被誉为交响乐之父，他的音乐至今依然持续娱乐和启发世人。

---

commission *n.* 授权；委托　　　　　immensely *adv.* 极大地；非常
conqueror *n.* 征服者

14

Gustavo Dudamel — the New Face of Classical Music

With arms waving and hair *bouncing*, Gustavo Dudamel excites crowds with his unique conducting style. Children, young people and adults all respond to his energy and *enthusiasm*. As a result, Dudamel is doing something others

Gustavo Dudamel

古典乐坛新秀杜达美

古斯塔夫·杜达美双手挥动、头发弹跃着，独特的指挥风格激起了群众的兴奋之情。无论是小孩、年轻人或成人全都会对他充沛的精力和热情产生共鸣，也因此杜达美得以办到前人做不到的事——那就是让古典音乐变得酷极了。

---

bounce *v.* 反弹；弹起   enthusiasm *n.* 热情

MCGRAW-HILL

before him have been unable to do. He's making classical music cool.

His early years

The 29-year-old conductor was born in Barquisimeto, Venezuela, on January 26, 1981. His parents, who are both musicians, began teaching Dudamel about music before he could talk. He was a *willing* student. While Dudamel was still quite little, his mother gave him a set of toy soldiers. But instead of preparing them for battle, the young boy arranged them into an orchestra. Then he began to *conduct* them. Music clearly was already his passion.

His formal studies began at 5 when Dudamel began studying music in Venezuela's orchestra for children. He started by singing in the chorus but soon began playing the violin. Conducting came at

---

早年生活

这位29岁的指挥家在1981年1月26日出生于委内瑞拉的巴尔基西梅托。他的双亲都是音乐家,在他还不会说话的时候,就开始教他音乐了,而他也是个乐意学习的学生。在杜达美还很小的时候,妈妈给了他一组玩具兵,可是他并不准备让玩具兵互相打斗,而是把它们组成管弦乐团,然后开始指挥了起来,音乐显然早就是他的爱好了。

杜达美5岁时开始在委内瑞拉的儿童管弦乐团学习音乐,从此展开正式的研习生涯。他一开始本来是在合唱团唱歌,但很快就开始拉小提琴,

---

willing *adj.* 乐意的;愿意的   conduct *v.* 指挥

15. And each new teacher spotted the boy's extraordinary talent.

At 17, Dudamel became the music director of the same orchestra he had grown up in. In 2004, he traveled to Germany for a conducting competition where he won first place. One of the judges was Esa-Pekka Salonen, then director of the Los Angeles Philharmonic Orchestra. With great excitement, Salonen contacted orchestra president Deborah Borda about this amazing young musician. Wasting no time, she booked Dudamel for his U.S. *debut*. Other invitations also arrived from Israel, Stockholm and London, and Dudamel's life changed forever.

并在15岁时开始指挥，而每一位教他的新老师都注意到他的特殊天赋。

　　杜达美就在委内瑞拉的儿童管弦乐团中逐渐成长，并在17岁时成为这个乐团的音乐总监。2004年，他到德国参加指挥大赛，并获得第一名，而其中有位评审是当时洛杉矶爱乐管弦乐团的（音乐）总监沙隆能。沙隆能异常兴奋地和洛杉矶爱乐的（行政）总监博达联络，告知有关这位令人惊奇的年轻音乐家的消息，于是博达毫不迟疑地约定让杜达美在美国首次登台，此外还有其他来自以色列、斯德哥尔摩和伦敦等地的邀约，杜达美的人生于是永久改变了。

---

debut *n.* 首次亮相；初次登台

The move to Los Angeles

Borda continued watching Dudamel with interest. Eventually, her orchestra invited him to become its music director following Salonen's *retirement*.

On October 3, 2009, an all-day free event introduced Dudamel to the city. Eighteen thousand people arrived, watching enthusiastically for the trademark smile and flying hair. Dudamel's performance didn't disappoint them, bringing the cheering crowd to its feet repeatedly. Fireworks spelled out his name in the sky as the music world declared its latest star.

转换到洛杉矶

博达持续关注杜达美。最后，她的管弦乐团在沙隆能退休后邀请杜达美接任音乐总监。

在2009年10月3号，一项免费的全天活动把杜达美介绍给洛杉矶市，共有18,000人到场（出席这项活动），他们满怀热忱地望着杜达美正字标记的微笑和飞扬的头发，而杜达美的表现也没有让他们失望。他使得喝彩的群众一再起立叫好。烟火在空中拼出了他的名字——音乐界就此宣布杜达美为乐坛新星。

---

retirement *n.* 退休

15

Life With Louisa

Many notable author's dig deep into their *imaginations* or search far and wide to find inspiration for their stories. Louisa May Alcott (1832-1888), however, didn't have to look much further than her family.

Louisa May Alcott

Growing up

The second of four daughters born to Amos Bronson and Abigail May Alcott, Alcott had a childhood that

---

小妇人的真实人生

许多知名作家都曾为了寻找故事的灵感，而深入挖掘自己的想象或四处搜寻。但路易莎·梅·爱尔考特（1832—1888年）却不需要在自己的家庭之外苦苦寻找故事灵感。

她的成长

爱默斯·布朗森·爱尔考特和爱碧凯尔·梅·爱尔考特共生了4个女儿，其中路易莎·梅·爱尔考特排行老二，而她的童年和一般孩子大不相

---

imagination *n.* 想象；想象力

was far from typical. She and her three sisters, Anna, Elizabeth and May, were educated by their deeply *philosophical* father and raised to practice "plain living and high thinking." Simplicity came in the form of *communal* living, where Alcott learned to *abstain* from eating meat and animal products, drink only water, and bathe in unheated water. As for high thinking, Alcott was regularly enlightened by family friends and American literary greats Ralph Waldo Emerson, Henry David Thoreau and Nathaniel Hawthorne. Frequent visits to Emerson's vast library, walks into nature with Thoreau and intellectual insight from Hawthorne inspired and influenced Alcott a great deal.

Alcott's surrounded by such *passionate* and knowledgeable authors, Alcott developed an early love for writing. With her rich imagination, this self-proclaimed tomboy penned stories she and her sisters would later act out for friends.

同。她和三个姊妹安娜、伊丽莎白和梅受教于深富哲思的父亲，教养方式是要她们力行"简朴生活、崇高思想"。简朴生活是透过共同的小区生活的形式来进行，这让路易莎学到不吃肉或动物制品，只喝水、用未加热的水洗澡等。至于崇高思想，则是定期接受家中友人暨美国文学巨擘埃默森、梭罗和霍桑等人的启发。她经常造访埃默森藏书丰富的图书馆，也和梭罗一起走入大自然，还从霍桑那里学习到知性洞见，这些经历都大大启发、影响了她。

周遭有这些热情、博学的作家，也让她很早就开始热爱写作。由于想象力丰富，于是这位自认很男孩子气的女孩便提笔写下了自己和姊妹们的故事，后来她们还为朋友表演这些故事。

---

philosophical *adj.* 哲学的

communal *adj.* 公用的；公共的

abstain *v.* 戒；戒除

passionate *adj.* 热情的；狂热的

When poverty began to plague her family, 15-year-old Alcott *pledged* to help, proclaiming, "I'll be rich and famous and happy before I die, see if I won't!"

Determined to keep her promise to help her family, Alcott began contributing to the family's income almost immediately. To do so, she worked as a teacher, *seamstress* and servant, all the while continuing to write.

When the American Civil War broke out, Alcott enlisted as a nurse. One year later, *Hospital Sketches* (1863) was published detailing her experiences and *propelling* Alcott into the *limelight*.

Little Women

When her publisher requested that Alcott write a book for girls, the 35-year-old author penned *Little Women* (1868). What would

---

后来她的家境转为贫困，于是15岁的路易莎便誓言要帮忙，宣称"在我死之前，一定要变得富有、成名又快乐，我一定能做到！"

她决定要信守帮忙家境的诺言，而且几乎立刻就对家境有所贡献了。为了帮忙家计，她担任过教师、女裁缝和仆人，其间还一直持续写作。

美国爆发内战后，她加入护士的行列，一年后出版了细述自己经历的《医院素描》（1863年），这版书使她成为众所瞩目的焦点。

《小妇人》

后来她的出版商要求她为女孩子写一本书，于是这位35岁的作家便写下了《小妇人》（1868年）。《小妇人》很快成为她最有名的作品，

---

pledge *v.* 保证；发誓　　　　seamstress *n.* 女裁缝
propel *v.* 驱动；推进　　　　limelight *n.* 公众注目的中心

quickly become her most famous novel, *Little Women* is a fictional piece based on the lives of Alcott and her family. Alcott's life is represented by the novel's strongwilled and independent *protagonist* Jo March. Throughout the novel, Jo and her sisters enjoy exciting adventures together, no doubt similar to what Alcott would have experienced with her sisters.

Today, Alcott's life continues to live on through her fiction. *Little Women* is now considered a classic and has even gone on to inspire several film adaptations along the way.

这是部以她和家人为蓝本的小说。小说中意志坚强又独立自主的主人翁乔·马其再现了路易莎·梅·爱尔考特的生活。在整部小说中，乔和姊妹一起享受精彩有趣的冒险，这无疑和路易莎及其姊妹的亲身经历类似。

现在路易莎·梅·爱尔考特的生活点滴透过她的小说继续长存，《小妇人》如今被视为经典作品，甚至成为电影灵感来源，持续被改编成好几部电影。

---

protagonist *n.* 主人公；主角

16

Nicolaus Copernicus: Moving Astronomy Forward

Nicolaus Copernicus (1473-1543) changed the world by *challenging* the common beliefs of his time. He completely *altered* the way people thought about their world and the universe. Thanks to Copernicus' *theories*, the entire Western world began to shift its *perspective*

Nicolaus Copernicus

哥白尼的天文革命

尼可拉斯·哥白尼（生于1473年，卒于1543年）藉由挑战当时很普遍的信念而改变了全世界。他彻底改变了人们对世界以及宇宙的思考模式，而多亏了哥白尼的理论，整个西方世界才开始将其观点从一个以地球为中心的宇宙，改为以太阳为中心的体系。

---

challenge *v.* 挑战
theory *n.* 理论

alter *v.* 改变
perspective *n.* 观点

from an Earth-centered universe to a sun-centered system.

The broadly educated student

Copernicus was born into a wealthy *merchant* family in Poland in 1473. When his father died, 10-year-old Copernicus moved in with his uncle, who later became a Roman Catholic *bishop*. While raising Copernicus, his uncle directed both the boy's advancement in the church and his education.

Copernicus began his university studies at the University of Cracow where mathematics, *astronomy* and *astrology* sparked his interest. But he left before finishing his degree, as was common at the time, and went to work for the church in Frombork. Then he followed in his uncle's footsteps by studying at the University of Bologna. While there, he lived with Domenico Maria Novara,

---

博学多闻的学生

哥白尼于1473年诞生于波兰富商之家。父亲过世后，10岁的哥白尼搬到舅舅家，他的舅舅后来成为天主教会的主教，而舅舅养育哥白尼的方式，是让他在教会和接受教育两方面同时并进。

哥白尼在克拉科大学展开大学课业，而他也开始对数学、天文学和占星学产生兴趣。不过他在拿到学位之前就暂离大学，而到弗劳恩堡的教会工作，这种做法在当时相当普遍。之后他追随舅舅的脚步到波隆那大学读书。在那里时，他和学校首席天文学教授多米尼克·马利亚·诺瓦拉同住。在那个时代里，托勒密仍被视为地位最崇高的天文学家，而当时他

---

merchant *n.* 商人

astronomy *n.* 天文学

bishop *n.* 主教

astrology *n.* 占星学

the school's chief astronomy professor. Novara was probably the first person Copernicus had ever met who dared to challenge the 1,400-year-old conclusions of that era's *paramount* astronomer: Ptolemy.

From Bologna, Copernicus went on to the University of Padua to study medicine, which at the time was closely linked to astrology. While studying how the movements of the heavens' *spheres* affected a person's health, Copernicus became an expert on the night sky.

Settling at the University of Ferrara, his fourth and final university, Copernicus *obtained* his first and only degree: a doctorate in canon law. With his broad education completed, Copernicus returned to Frombork in 1510 to resume his duties with the church.

（以地球为宇宙中心）的推论已经有1400年的历史了；在哥白尼遇见过的人当中，诺瓦拉大概是第一个敢于挑战托勒密推论的人。

哥白尼继波隆那之后继续前往帕度亚大学研习医学，医学在当时和占星学有密切关连。哥白尼研究天体运行如何影响一个人的健康，并成了夜空的专家。

哥白尼后来在费拉拉大学安顿下来，那是他就读的第四所也是最后一所大学，后来获得了生平第一个也是唯一的学位：教会法规博士。哥白尼完成了广博的教育，在1510年回到弗劳恩堡重拾他在教会的职务。

paramount *adj.* 至为重要的
obtain *v.* 得到；获得

sphere *n.* 球体；球形

The revolutionary astronomer

In Copernicus' day, Europe believed the Earth sat *motionless* at the center of the universe. People were convinced the sun, the moon and planets *revolved* around the Earth, and the second-century Greek astronomer Ptolemy had "proven" it with mathematics.

Although busy with church work, Copernicus made time for his scientific work, finding several problems with Ptolemy's Earth-centered model. More *significantly*, Copernicus found that a sun-centered model with a revolving Earth fit the data much better.

Although centuries of tradition and *superstition* suggested otherwise, mathematical calculations convinced Copernicus that Earth was not fixed at the universe's center. Instead, he realized Earth moved with the other planets in yearly revolutions around the sun.

富有革命性的天文学家

在哥白尼那个时代，欧洲人仍相信地球是静止不动地位于宇宙的中心，人们深信太阳、月亮和行星绕着地球转动，而公元二世纪的希腊天文学家托勒密用数学"证明"了这个观念。

哥白尼虽然忙于教会的工作，却仍抽空从事科学研究，并在托勒密的地球中心说模型里发现了一些问题。更重要的是，哥白尼发现，以太阳为中心的模型加上环绕（太阳）运行的地球，才更符合数据。

尽管几世纪以来的传统与迷信持不同的看法，但数学计算的结果使哥白尼确信地球并非固定在宇宙的中心，相反地，他发现地球和其他行星其实会一年一度地环绕太阳运行。

---

motionless　*adj.*　静止的　　　　　　　　revolve　*v.*　旋转；转动
significantly　*adv.*　重要地　　　　　　　superstition　*n.*　迷信

While his conclusions would answer astronomers' questions, Copernicus was well aware that "moving the Earth" would shake the *foundations* of everyone else's worldview. So sometime before 1514, he carefully *revealed* his conclusions, gradually introducing them in an essay he sent only to various colleagues in *philosophy* and astronomy. Over the next several years, he *refined* his results while his theory circulated around Europe, spreading his reputation as a remarkable astronomer.

In 1539, a young mathematician named Georg Rheticus came to study under the seasoned 66-year-old astronomer. Fascinated by his conclusions, Rheticus worked with Copernicus to publish an introduction to his sun-centered universe model. Its success pushed Copernicus to complete and publish his entire, massive six-volume

虽然哥白尼的推论能解答天文学家的疑惑，但他也很清楚"移动地球"将会撼动所有其他人世界观的基础。于是他大约在1514年之前，开始小心翼翼地揭露他的推论，逐步渐进地在一篇论文中先加以介绍，而那篇论文他只寄给哲学与天文学界的几位同事。在接下来的几年里，他修正自己的研究成果使更臻完善，而他的理论在欧洲也渐渐流传，于是他身为杰出天文学家的声望就此传开。

1539年，一位名叫乔治·瑞提克斯的年轻数学家来到这位时年66岁、经验丰富的天文学家门下求教。瑞提克斯深受哥白尼的推论所吸引，并和他合作出版介绍哥白尼以太阳为中心的宇宙模型的导论，导论的成功

foundation *n.* 基础
philosophy *n.* 哲学

reveal *v.* 揭露
refine *v.* 改善；改进

work, *On the Revolutions of the Heavenly Spheres*, at the end of his life. *Legend* holds that Copernicus held a published copy of his life's work on his deathbed on May 24, 1543.

In *subsequent* years, astronomers built upon Copernicus' conclusions, continuing to challenge the previous perspective. By the 1700s, it was nearly impossible to find an astronomer who wasn't convinced of the Copernican model's *accuracy*. Copernicus' impact on both astronomy and how we pursue knowledge today has truly been *astronomical*.

也促使哥白尼得以在辞世前完成并完整出版他的作品，那就是厚达6册的《天体运行论》。根据传说，哥白尼于1543年5月24日临终之际，手里还拿着一本已出版的毕生心血结晶。

在之后几年里，天文学家继续以哥白尼的推论为基础，来挑战以往的观点。到了18世纪时，就几乎已找不到任何天文学家不相信哥白尼模型的正确性了。哥白尼对天文学及人类如今追求知识的方式的影响，实在异常巨大。

---

legend *n.* 传说
accuracy *n.* 精确（性）；精准（性）

subsequent *adj.* 随后的
astronomical *adj.* 极其巨大的

17

Confucius: His Wisdom Lives On

Zhuangzi（庄子）once *characterized* Confucius as saying, "You may forget me as I once was, but there is something *unforgettable* about me that will still live on." This prediction remains *accurate* as Confucius' words still live on today and have been *quoted* by people down through the ages. Because of the writings and

CONFUCIUS

孔子：智慧永存

庄子曾描述孔子说："虽忘乎故吾，吾有不忘者存。"（译注：出自《庄子》外篇之〈田子方〉）这个预言一点也没错，因为孔子的金玉良言仍流传至今，为世世代代的人不断引用，而他遗留给世人的著作与学说，使其被公认为史上最有智慧的人士之一。

---

characterize *v.* 描述
accurate *adj.* 精确的

unforgettable *adj.* 令人难忘的
quote *v.* 引用

teachings he left behind, Confucius is considered one of the history's wisest men.

Childhood through early manhood

When he was born in 551 B.C. in Lu（鲁）, China, the baby who would someday be called Kong Fuzi（孔夫子）was named Kong Qiu（孔丘）. Confucius' father, Kong Shuliang（孔叔梁）, was a *descendant* of the royal family of Shang and had at one time been governor of the town of Zou（邹）. When Kong Qiu was three years old, his father died, leaving the child and his young mother in poverty. As Kong Qiu grew older, their *financial* situation required him to take on *menial* jobs such as caring for livestock. He became known as a polite, smart and hard-working young man with an *insatiable* desire to learn. This thirst for knowledge would push him toward a life of learning and teaching others.

Confucius married when he was 19, had a son and two

孩提时代至青年时期

公元前551年，孔子诞生于鲁国，这名未来将成为孔夫子的婴孩被取名为孔丘。孔子的父亲孔叔梁纥为商朝王室后裔，也曾治理过邹邑。孔丘3岁时，父亲去世，独留他与年纪尚轻的母亲贫苦度日。孔丘渐长，鉴于家中经济困顿，而从事卑微的工作，如看顾牲畜。后来他成为大家眼中有礼貌、聪明又勤奋上进的年轻人，而且有永无止尽的求知欲。求知若渴促使孔子以教、学为终生志业。

孔子19岁结婚，生下一男二女。他不断从事各种工作，也曾在地方

---

descendant *n.* 后裔
menial *adj.* 报酬低的

financial *adj.* 经济的
insatiable *adj.* 无法满足的

daughters, and continued working assorted jobs, including several in his local government. Around the age of 30, Confucius began his teaching career, sometimes traveling from town to town while teaching a group of students who *accompanied* him. As a result, it didn't take long for his principles to spread and for others to begin recognizing him for the wise *sage* that he was.

Times of chaos and wandering

Confucius became increasingly *distressed* by the political corruption and disorder in society, so he decided to get involved in politics, hoping to make a difference. He secured a position as the Minister of Justice in Lu, but after realizing that his policies and ideas weren't being accepted, he left the post, disheartened.

The philosopher truly believed that society and governments would improve if they would follow the great moral teachings of

---

政府做过几项差事。30岁左右，孔子开始以教学为业，有时遍访各邑，同时教导跟随他的一群学生。结果不出多久，他的信条就传播开来，世人开始把孔子视为圣人。

乱世漂泊

孔子对政治腐败与社会动乱愈来愈感到沉痛，于是决定涉入政治，以期改变现况。他在鲁国担任了相当于如今的司法部长的大司寇，但后来了解到自己的政策与理念不见容于当政，便辞去官位，沮丧灰心不已。

这位哲人衷心相信，只要遵循过去伟大的道德教诲，就能改善社会与政府。因此孔子便在公元前496年起开始四处游历，找寻愿意采纳他的伦

---

accompany *v.* 陪伴
distressed *adj.* 痛苦的；苦恼的

sage *n.* 圣人；智者

the past. So, in 496 B.C. Confucius began a period of wandering in search of a ruler who would adopt his ethical teachings. For the next 12 years, Confucius and a growing group of *disciples* traveled from town to town advising rulers and local officials.

Throughout his 12-year-journey, Confucius *encountered* indifference, extreme hardship and danger, nearly being *assassinated* on one occasion. At 67, he returned to Lu, having been unsuccessful in his efforts to persuade even one ruler to practice his moral *doctrines*. Yet Confucius never faltered in his belief that the most important task of any ruler was to work for the welfare and happiness of his people.

Confucius' final years

He spent the next few years studying, writing and teaching his

---

理学说的明君。往后12年，孔子与一群数量渐增的学生周游列国，向君主与地方官员提出建言。

在12年的旅程中，孔子曾遭人冷漠以待，也曾面临极端的磨难，并身陷险境，有次甚至差点遭人暗杀。孔子67岁时返回鲁国，心血尽付流水，没有一位君主接受劝服采用他的道德学说。然而孔子从不怀疑自己的信念：君主的首要任务就是为人民谋福祉。

孔子的晚年

接下来几年，孔子致力于研究、写作，也教导不断增加的学生。据说

---

disciple *n.* 门徒；信徒

assassinate *v.* 暗杀

encounter *v.* 遭遇

doctrine *n.* 学说

ever-expanding group of students. It's been said that up to 3,000 men may have studied with Confucius although only 22 are actually mentioned in the Analects, which were written by his disciples.

Sadly, Confucius' last years were unhappy, as his son died during this time and his favorite disciple died the year the philosopher returned to Lu. One morning in 479 B.C., the sage died in bed. His followers buried him with great *ceremony*, built huts close to his *grave*, and spent the next three years there in *mournful* respect.

The news of his death spread quickly, and finally in death, Confucius received national respect and boundless admiration — admiration that continues today for China's greatest teacher.

有3000名学生曾受教于孔子，但由孔子弟子写成的《论语》中，明确提到的弟子人数仅有22名。

令人感伤的是，孔子晚年过得并不快乐，不仅儿子去世，他最喜爱的弟子也在他回到鲁国的那年离开人世。公元前479年的一天早晨，这位圣人在卧榻上辞世。孔子的追随者举行盛大的葬礼，并在他的墓旁搭建茅屋，守丧3年。

孔子的死讯迅速传开。孔子离开人世后，终于获得全民的敬仰及无限钦佩。时至今日，这位中国最伟大的教师仍为世人所敬佩。

---

ceremony *n.* 仪式　　　　　　　　　　　　　　　　grave *n.* 坟墓
mournful *adj.* 悲痛的

18

Chopin: Poet of the Piano

On a winter night in 1810, a boy with *exceptional* talent was born in a village in Poland. Son of a French father and Polish mother, Frédéric François Chopin (1810-1849) would end up writing *expressive* piano music that still moves audiences today.

The youth in Poland

Chopin began studying the piano at home when he was 5. His *prodigious* talent quickly became obvious. Before he was 10, Chopin

---

钢琴诗人肖邦

1810年的一个冬夜，一名才华出众的男孩诞生在波兰一座村庄里。父亲是法国人、母亲是波兰人的弗雷德里克·弗朗索瓦·肖邦（1810—1849年）终将会创作出富含感情的钢琴乐曲，至今依然感动着听众。

波兰的青年时期

肖邦5岁时开始在家里学钢琴，他非凡的才华很快地彰显出来。肖邦不到10岁时，就已经开始作曲及公开演奏。他7岁时发表第一首音乐作

---

exceptional *adj.* 杰出的；优秀的
prodigious *adj.* 巨大的；伟大的

expressive *adj.* 富于表情的

was *composing* music and performing in public. He published his first composition at the age of 7. At 11, he performed his own music for Alexander I, the tsar of Russia. The pleased tsar gave Chopin a diamond ring.

Chopin benefited from studying under teachers that encouraged his original style and didn't push him to follow traditional *conventions*. Chopin's teachers *emphasized* classical composers such as Beethoven and Mozart without neglecting to introduce Chopin to *contemporary* romantic composers. By age 20, Chopin had already composed many piano pieces, including Polish folk dances called polonaises and mazurkas. In 1830, Chopin embarked on a music tour that eventually took him to Paris.

品；11岁时，为俄国沙皇亚历山大一世演奏自己所作的乐曲，龙心大悦的沙皇还赠与他一只钻戒。

肖邦的指导老师鼓励他发展原创风格，不会强迫他遵循传统常规，让他受益良多。肖邦的老师重视贝多芬及莫扎特等古典作曲家，但也没有忽略让肖邦接触当代的浪漫主义作曲家。到了20岁时，肖邦已经创作了许多钢琴乐曲，包括称为波兰舞曲及玛祖卡舞曲的波兰民间舞蹈乐曲。1830年，肖邦展开音乐巡回演出，最后来到了巴黎。

---

compose *v.* 作曲；创作　　　　　　convention *n.* 常规；惯例
emphasize *v.* 强调　　　　　　　　contemporary *adj.* 当代的；现代的

The composer in Paris

In 1831, Chopin *settled down* in Paris, making a living as a composer and highly paid piano teacher. Shy by nature, Chopin avoided playing in public, preferring to perform for small groups instead. His health also began declining during this time.

In 1838, he spent the winter in Majorca, an island south of Spain. Chopin was forced out of an apartment there because the landlord feared he had *tuberculosis*. Though the move was a hardship, Chopin managed to compose 24 pieces of music, called *preludes*, that winter.

在巴黎的作曲家

1831年，肖邦在巴黎定居下来，以担任作曲家及薪资优渥的钢琴老师谋生。肖邦天性害羞，所以尽量避免公开演出，比较喜欢为小团体演奏。在这段时期，他的健康情形也开始逐渐恶化。

1838年，肖邦到西班牙南方的马约卡岛过冬，后来却被强迫搬出公寓，因为房东担心他得了肺结核。虽然搬家是件苦差事，但肖邦在那年冬天仍努力创作了24首乐曲，被称为前奏曲。

---

settle down 定居

prelude *n.* 序曲；前奏曲

tuberculosis *n.* 肺结核

Despite his poor health, Chopin was *dedicated* to composing. An observer once described his creative process. "[The music] came to his piano suddenly … or it sang in his head during a walk. … But then would begin the most *heartbreaking* labor I have ever *witnessed*. … He would shut himself up in his room for days at a time, weeping, pacing, breaking his pens, repeating and changing a single measure a hundred times."

In 1849, Chopin's ill health finally took his life. However, through Chopin's more than 200 compositions, his passion can still be heard from the piano.

肖邦尽管体弱多病，还是用心投入音乐创作。一名旁观友人曾经如此描述他的创作过程："音乐突然从他的钢琴流泻出来……或是在他散步时在脑中响起……但接着就开始我所见过最令人心酸的艰苦过程……他会把自己关在房间里，一次连续好几天，时而啜泣、时而来回踱步、写到笔都折断了，不断重复和修改单一小节，多达上百次。"

1849年，肖邦的病体终于宣告不治。然而，透过肖邦200首以上的音乐作品，我们依然可以藉由钢琴而聆听到他的热情。

---

dedicated *adj.* 专心致志的　　　　heartbreaking *adj.* 令人心碎的
witness *v.* 见证

19

Daniel Craig: From Stage to Screen

Like many little boys in the 1970s, Daniel Craig dreamed of being James Bond, but as an adult actor, he never *aspired* to play the part. Yet it was this very role as the famous secret agent that turned Craig into a Hollywood superstar.

从舞台跃上银幕的丹尼尔·克雷格

就和20世纪70年代的许多小男孩一样，丹尼尔·克雷格也梦想成为詹姆士·邦德，不过等到他成为成人演员时，却从未渴求饰演这个角色。然而，正是演出这个知名情报员的角色，让克雷格成为好莱坞的超级巨星。

---

aspire *v.* 渴望

A young star in the making

Craig was born in 1968 in Chester, England, to parents Tim and Olivia Craig. His mother, who at one time had acting *aspirations*, *exposed* her son to *theatrical* productions at a very young age. It came as no surprise when Craig earned his very first role at age 6 in his primary school's production of the musical *Oliver*. Soon after, Craig accompanied his father to see his first Bond movie, and the impact of the two experiences resulted in his catching the acting bug!

He might not have been a great student, but according to his high school drama teacher Hilary Green, he was one of the school's best actors. She said that it was clear from his very first *audition* that "he was a natural on the stage … and quite exceptional."

年少的明日之星

克雷格于1968年生于英国的切斯特，父母亲是蒂姆和奥莉维亚·克雷格。他母亲一度向往演戏，并让儿子在很小的时候就接触戏剧表演。毫不令人意外地，克雷格6岁时便在他就读的小学所演出的音乐剧《孤雏泪》中获得生平第一个角色。不久之后，克雷格首次和父亲一起去看邦德电影，这两次经验的影响使他开始对演戏着迷。

他也许不是个优秀的学生，但据他的中学戏剧老师希拉里·格林表示，他是该中学最杰出的演员之一。她表示，从他第一次试演就清楚可见"他有站上舞台的表演天分……而且相当出色。"

---

aspiration *n.* 渴望；志向　　　　　　　expose *v.* 使接触；使体验
theatrical *adj.* 戏剧的　　　　　　　　audition *n.* 试演

Others must have agreed because at age 16 Craig auditioned and was accepted into London's National Youth Theater (NYT).

Craig later graduated from London's *premier* academy, the Guildhall School of Music and Drama. In 1992, he made his professional *debut* in the film *The Power of One*. He kept busy over the next 14 years, taking on over 50 roles and *amassing* an impressive résumé.

The Blonde Bond

One of those roles caught the eye of movie producer Barbara Broccoli, who had just begun looking for someone to replace Pierce Brosnan as James Bond. Broccoli said that when she saw Craig on

---

其他人想必也同意她的看法，因为克雷格16岁时就到伦敦国家青年剧团（简称NYT）试演并获录取。

克雷格后来毕业于伦敦一流的市政厅音乐戏剧学院。1992年，他在《小子要自强》这部电影中首次职业演出。在其后的14年里，他一直忙于工作，接演过50多个角色，累积了可观的资历。

金发邦德

其中一个角色吸引了电影制作人芭芭拉·布罗柯里的目光，她当时刚开始寻找接替皮尔斯·布洛斯南演出詹姆士·邦德的人选。布罗柯里说，当她看见银幕上的克雷格时，她看见自己心目中的邦德正与她四目相望。

---

premier *adj.* 最著名的；第一的   debut *n.* 初次登台
amass *v.* 积累

the screen, she saw her Bond staring back at her.

Though she was convinced, Craig wasn't so sure. He had already earned the reputation as a serious, *credible* actor, and he knew that taking on the role of Bond could be a *gamble*. Craig accepted the part, though, and the gamble paid off as his first Bond film, *Casino Royale*, earned $594,239,066, becoming the highest-grossing Bond film in the franchise.

Craig once said, "I always wanted to be an actor. I had the *arrogance* to believe I couldn't be anything else." Whether it is arrogance or *determination*, his fans are glad he hasn't let anything stand in the way of his acting career.

虽然她对克雷格适合扮演邦德深信不疑，但克雷格自己却不太确定。他当时已经赢得身为严肃、可靠的演员的名声，深知接下邦德一角可能很冒险。然而克雷格接受了这个角色，最后证明这场冒险是值得的，因为他的第一部邦德电影《007首部曲：皇家夜总会》赚进了594,239,066美元，成为票房收益最高的邦德电影。

克雷格曾说："我一向想成为演员。我有那种傲慢，认为自己不可能做别的事。"不论那是出于傲慢还是决心，他的影迷都很高兴他不曾让任何事物阻碍他的演艺生涯。

---

credible *adj.* 可靠的；可信的　　　　gamble *n.* 赌博；冒险
arrogance *n.* 傲慢　　　　　　　　determination *n.* 决心

20

Behind the Scenes With Sandra

In just 20 years, Sandra Bullock has been an *undercover* FBI agent, a *homicide* detective and a bus driver who saves the day. But it's not just her popular movie roles that have earned the 46-year-old actress scores of adoring fans. Off screen she has been commended for her girl-next-door smile, her down-to-earth *approachability*, her generous, *philanthropic* spirit and her likeable personality. Known as "America's

Sandra Bullock

荧屏幕后的桑德拉·布洛克

仅20年内,桑德拉·布洛克就当过美国联邦调查局卧底干员、凶杀案警探和扭转局势的公交车司机;不过,这位46岁的女演员不仅仅是靠这些受人欢迎的电影角色,才赢得众多影迷的崇拜,因为荧屏幕后的她,那邻家女孩的笑容、实实在在平易近人的特质、慷慨行善的精神以及讨人喜欢的个性,实在令她备受赞誉。有"美国甜心"之称的布

---

undercover *adj.* 私下进行的;暗中做的
approachability *n.* 可接近;易接近

homicide *n.* 杀人罪
philanthropic *adj.* 慈善的

Sweetheart," Bullock is one Hollywood star that shines brightly.

Growing up

Born to a German, opera-singing mother and an American, vocal coach father, Bullock grew up around talent. Having performers for parents *nurtured* her creative drive and *propelled* her onto the stage. By age 12, Bullock was singing in a children's choir and studying ballet in Nuremberg, Germany, where her family lived at the time. During these years, Bullock also *accompanied* her mother on several opera tours throughout Europe. All the while, her passion for performance was growing.

When her family returned to the United States, Bullock completed high school and *enrolled* in a university. Three credits short of graduation, however, Bullock left school and headed to New York in 1986 to pursue her dream of becoming an actress.

洛克，是颗耀眼的好莱坞明星。

成长背景

母亲是德国歌剧演唱家，父亲是美国声乐教练，布洛克成长过程中，身边围绕着才华横溢的人。双亲皆为表演者，培养出她的创造力，也驱使她踏上舞台。布洛克12岁参加儿童合唱团，并在当时全家旅居的德国纽伦堡学芭蕾。那些年期间，布洛克也陪着母亲参加好几次欧洲歌剧巡演。一直以来，她对表演的热诚愈来愈强烈。

布洛克随家人搬回美国，高中毕业便进入大学就读。只差三学分就能毕业，她却在1986年辍学前往纽约追寻当女演员的梦想。

---

nurture *v.* 培养   propel *v.* 驱使；迫使

accompany *v.* 陪伴   enroll *v.* 登记；注册

At home in Hollywood

Three years later with a few minor roles to her name, Bullock left New York for Los Angeles in hopes of finding success in Hollywood. She finally got her big break when she co-starred in 1994's action-packed *thriller Speed*. Soon after, Sandra Bullock became both a household name and sought-after actress. Movie-role offers poured in, and Bullock's *celebrity soared*. Fans and critics alike praised Bullock's *versatility* as an actress.

After a string of successful films including *While You Were Sleeping*, *Miss Congeniality*, *Hope Floats* and the award-winning *Crash*, Bullock received the opportunity of a lifetime. And she almost turned it down.

闯荡好莱坞如鱼得水

布洛克在纽约待了3年，演过一些小角色，后来便前往洛杉矶，希望能在好莱坞闯出一番名堂。终于在1994年，她联袂主演紧张刺激的动作片《捍卫战警》，事业才大有斩获。不久后，桑德拉·布洛克就成为家喻户晓、电影公司争相邀请的女星。片约如雪片般飞来，布洛克声名鹊起。影迷与影评人都称赞布洛克是位多才多艺的女演员。

布洛克主演的佳片连连，如《二见钟情》、《麻辣女王》、《真爱告白》以及得奖作品《冲击效应》，后来得到了一个千载难逢的演出机会，但她却差点婉拒。

---

thriller *n.* 惊险电影　　　　　　　　celebrity *n.* 名誉；声望
soar *v.* 急升；猛增　　　　　　　　versatility *n.* 多才多艺

Bullock gets blindsided

Bullock was initially terrified of *portraying* Leigh Anne Tuohy, the woman whose true story is the basis of the highly *acclaimed* film *The Blind Side*. Bullock didn't know if she could do justice to the demanding role. Finally, after nearly a year of trying to persuade her, the film's director convinced Bullock to take the role. Bullock wowed both critics and fans with her performance and went on to win 2010's *coveted* Academy Award for Best Actress. And with that, Bullock's star shines more brightly than ever.

布洛克被攻其不备

大获好评的电影《攻其不备》是以黎·安·杜希的真实故事改编而成，起初，布洛克非常害怕饰演黎·安的角色。她不确定自己是否能把这个极具挑战性的角色诠释得恰如其分。最后，电影导演花了近一年的时间才说服布洛克接演。布洛克的演技令影评人与影迷惊艳，更在2010年得到了梦寐以求的奥斯卡最佳女主角奖。有了金奖加持，布洛克的星光比过去更加闪耀了。

---

portray *v.* 扮演　　　　　　　　　　　　acclaim *v.* 给予高度评价
covet *v.* 渴望

21

Mark Twain: "The Father of American Literature"

In 1835, the return of Halley's *comet* caused great excitement in the world. That same year in another *historic* event, the baby who would become the "Father of American Literature" was born.

Samuel Langhorne Clemens – known later as Mark Twain – began

MARK TWAIN

life on November 30, 1835, in Florida, Mo. When Clemens was

美国文学之父：马克·吐温

1835年，哈雷彗星重返地球引起举世轰动，而同年也发生了另一项历史性的事件，那就是日后将成为"美国文学之父"的婴儿诞生了。

萨缪尔·兰贺尔·克莱门斯，也就是日后为人所知的马克·吐温于1835年11月30日在密苏里州的佛罗里达诞生。克莱门斯4岁左右时，举家

---

comet *n.* 彗星　　　　　　　　　　　　　historic *adj.* 历史性的

around 4, his family moved to Hannibal, Mo., a river town *situated* on the Mississippi River. His new home provided him with lots of excitement and adventure as *steamboats* from New Orleans and St. Louis stopped there regularly. The new environment also proved to be *fertile* ground for a boy with an active imagination and a gift for storytelling.

Discovering his talent

When Clemens was only 11, his father died, leaving the family in financial difficulty. At 13, the boy had to quit school and find a job, working first for a printer. Next he worked for his brother, a newspaper publisher, and it was then that Clemens discovered how much he enjoyed writing. In his free time, he began writing and *submitting* humorous pieces to his brother 's newspaper.

搬迁至密苏里州的汉尼拔，那是坐落在密西西比河畔的市镇。他的新家带来许多刺激及冒险的经历，因为来自纽奥良及圣路易的汽船会定期在那儿停泊，而这个新环境也成为这个想象力丰富又有说故事天分的小男孩的乐土。

发现天分

克莱门斯年仅11岁时，父亲去世了，这使全家陷入财务困境。他在13岁时就不得不辍学找工作，起初，他为一位印刷商工作，接着则为身为报纸出版商的兄长工作，而克莱门斯就是在此时发现自己非常喜欢写作。他利用空闲时写作，并将自己所写的幽默作品投稿到兄长的报社。

---

situated *adj.* 坐落在；位于
fertile *adj.* 能产生好结果的；促进的

steamboat *n.* 汽船
submit *v.* 呈递；提交

Realizing a dream

Though Clemens liked writing, he had always dreamed of piloting steamboats on the *mighty* Mississippi River. While in his 20s, he decided to do it, training and then working as a riverboat captain for three years. His experiences left a lasting impression on him and even provided the pen name Mark Twain, which he would later use.

Finding fame

In 1863, Clemens began publishing regularly as Mark Twain, but fame *eluded* him. Then in 1865 he found success with his short story *"The Celebrated Jumping Frog of Calaveras County"*. However, it was his books about two boys growing up along the Mississippi

---

实现梦想

虽然克莱门斯喜欢写作，但他一直梦想着能在浩瀚的密西西比河上开汽船。他在二十几岁时决定付诸行动，并在受训后担任三年的江轮船长。这样的经验在他心里烙下难以磨灭的印象，甚至让他想到用马克·吐温当笔名（译注：Mark Twain中的twain是two的古字形式，mark则是指标记，在河中航行必须测深在线达到有两噚水深的标记才行）。

求取名声

1863年，克莱门斯开始定期以马克·吐温为笔名发表作品，但却与名气无缘。后来在1865年，他以短篇故事《卡拉韦拉斯郡驰名的跳蛙》

---

mighty *adj.* 巨大的；非凡的   elude *v.* 逃避；躲避

River that would bring him lasting *prominence*. *The Adventures of Tom Sawyer* and *The Adventures of Huckleberry Finn* introduced readers to a child's world of delightful adventures.

Living on

Twain published over 60 works during his lifetime. Then, as he himself had predicted, he died the same year Halley's comet returned – in 1910. One hundred years ago, the world lost a literary giant. But his words still live on in the lives of America's favorite *fictional* boys, Tom Sawyer and Huckleberry Finn.

（暂译）一举成名；然而，让他声名卓著历久不衰的著作，则是密西西比河畔两名男孩的成长故事。《汤姆历险记》及《顽童历险记》让读者见识到小孩子的精彩冒险世界。

永存不朽

吐温在世时共出版了六十余部作品。后来，正如他自己所预测的，他在哈雷慧星重返地球的同一年——也就是1910年，撒手人寰。一百年前，世界失去了一位文学巨擘，但他的字句话语依然活在美国最受喜爱的虚构男孩的生命中，他们就是汤姆·索耶及哈克贝利·费恩。

---

prominence *n.* 卓越；出名   fictional *adj.* 虚构的

22

Hannah Montana: "Tween" Queen

Without a doubt, Miley Cyrus reigns as Hollywood's "tween" queen. Her show, *Hannah Montana*, *debuted* in 2006 as the number one *cable* show for kids aged 6-14. Add to that success two chart-topping CDs, a sold-out concert tour and a number one movie. And she's not even 16 years old yet!

Miley Cyrus

"吞世代" 小天后孟汉纳

麦莉·赛勒斯无疑是叱咤好莱坞的 "吞世代" 天后。她主演的影集《孟汉纳》2006年首度上映就成为6至14岁孩童最喜爱的有线电视节目。除了这个成就，她还发行了两张排行榜冠军大碟、举办一次入场券销售一空的巡回演唱会，还拍了一部卖座冠军电影。她还未满16岁呢！

debut *n.* 首次亮相　　　　　　　　　cable *n.* 有线电视

Born in 1992 in Tennessee, Miley is the daughter of country singer-turned-actor Billy Ray Cyrus and his wife, Tish. Miley got an early start in acting, beginning with a small role on her father's TV show in 2003. Then at age 12, Miley's cool confidence helped her beat out 1,000 other girls to win the role of *Hannah Montana*.

On the Disney Channel show, Miley plays Miley Stewart, a sometimes-awkward ninth grade girl who *moonlights* as pop sensation Hannah Montana. Stewart keeps her rock star identity a secret from all but her family and closest friends. The show *emphasizes* family, friendship and respect, making it a hit not only with kids but also with adults. Miley's real father plays her dad on the show.

麦莉于1992年出生于田纳西州，是乡村歌手出身的演员比利雷·赛勒斯与妻子蒂雪之女。麦莉很小就开始演戏，最早于2003年在父亲的电视节目中出演一个小角色。接着，12岁的时候，麦莉的沉着又酷酷的自信台风帮她打败1000个女孩，夺得《孟汉纳》一角。

麦莉在这个迪斯尼频道的影集中饰演麦莉·史都华，这个九年级女孩时而笨手笨脚，时而摇身一变当起流行音乐天后孟汉纳。史都华对她的摇滚巨星身份保密到家，只有家人和最亲的朋友才知道。这部影集着眼于亲情、友情和尊重，因此不仅受到孩子欢迎，也风靡成人观众。麦莉真实世界的父亲也在影集中饰演她爸爸。

---

moonlight *v.* （暗中）兼职

emphasize *v.* 强调

In June 2007, Miley released the two-disc *album Hannah Montana 2/Meet Miley Cyrus*. One disc contains songs from the show. And the other serves as the star's debut album – with songs about love, teenage life and growing up. In October, Miley set out on a 54-date North American concert tour. During the tour, she performed songs as Hannah and as herself. The concerts were wildly popular – tickets for some *venues* sold out within minutes and 14 extra performances were added.

The tour's success *spurred* Disney to create a 3-D movie version of the concert. The film hit number one at the box office and earned over $31 million in just three days.

2007年6月，麦莉推出双碟专辑《孟汉纳2／遇见麦莉》。其中一张大碟收录《孟汉纳》影集中的歌曲，另一张则是这位明星的首张作品，收录多首以爱、青少年生活与成长为主题的歌曲。10月，麦莉展开长达54场的北美巡回演唱会。巡回演出期间，她有时以孟汉纳，有时以真正的身份进行演唱。演唱会大受欢迎，某些场次的座位几分钟内就售罄，后来还加演了14场之多。

这次巡回演出的佳绩激使"迪斯尼"公司着手制作演唱会的3D电影版。这部电影荣登票房冠军，短短3天就赚进超过31,000,000万美金。

---

album *n.* 唱片；专辑　　　　　　　　venue *n.* 聚会地点
spur *v.* 刺激；激励

Though Miley is a huge star, she sees herself as a regular girl. Her parents agree; they work hard to keep her *grounded*. Miley attends church with her family every week and does homework and household chores.

With a big-screen version of *Hannah Montana* coming out next year, this young star is sure to keep rising – but with her feet on the ground!

虽然贵为超级巨星，麦莉仍自认是个平凡女孩。她的双亲也这么认为；他们煞费苦心，要她脚踏实地地做人。麦莉每个星期都会和家人去教会做礼拜，也不忘做功课和家事。

随着《孟汉纳》将于明年搬上大银幕，这位新星一定会更上层楼，但也会脚踏实地！

grounded *adj.* 持有合理和现实态度的

23

The Jonas Brothers

Swooning females, screaming crowds and sold-out concerts keep life exciting for the Jonas Brothers these days. Yet Kevin, 21; Joe, 19; and Nick, 16, seem to take their newfound fame in *stride*.

A "Band of Brothers"

Though they've been famous for less than three years, the brothers have been performing for much longer.

强纳斯兄弟

这一阵子，兴奋到快要晕倒的女生、尖叫个不停的群众和门票销售一空的演唱会让"强纳斯兄弟"的生活一点都不无聊，可是21岁的凯文、19岁的乔和16岁的尼克好像仍轻松面对近来涌现的名气。

兄弟乐团

虽然成名不到三年，这三兄弟投入表演的时间比这段时间长很多，其实他们小时候就常在自家地下室为父母开演唱会呢。在乐团享受成名滋味

---

stride *n.* 进展；步伐

In fact, as little boys they frequently gave "concerts" for their parents in the family *basement*. Before becoming the famous band they are today, each boy had already *achieved* individual success. Nick had appeared in four *Broadway* plays, Joe had also performed on stage, and Kevin had done commercials. But it wasn't until the three brothers signed with Hollywood Records in 2006 that their careers hit the fast *track*.

Today, they have numerous hit songs, a White House performance, a sold-out European tour and a TV movie under their belts. They've even starred in their own Disney reality show called The Jonas Brothers: Living the Dream. But, unlike many well-known pop stars, this group is not your conventional boy band.

之前，三兄弟各人已小有成绩。尼克曾在四出百老汇舞台剧（译注：均为音乐剧）露脸，乔也曾登台演出，凯文还曾是广告明星呢，但直到2006年，这三兄弟跟好莱坞唱片签约，演艺事业才一飞冲天。

如今，他们走红的歌曲不计其数，还一度于白宫表演，欧洲巡回演唱会的门票销售一空，还拍过一部电视电影，他们甚至演出了自己的迪斯尼真人实境秀"强纳斯兄弟：梦想起飞"，不过，和许多流行界走红明星不同的是，这个团体不是你心目中的一般男声乐团。

---

basement *n.* 地下室
Broadway *n.* 百老汇

achieve *v.* 完成；达到
track *n.* 方向；路线

Good role models

These days when bad behavior defines many celebrities, the Jonas Brothers stand alone. Instead of smoking, drinking and doing drugs, they pray together, wear *purity* rings and play golf!

Teenage fans love their *upbeat* sound while parents appreciate their *wholesome* lyrics and positive messages. These *ingredients* have helped to make the Jonas Brothers one of the most popular pop-rock bands around.

Charitable hearts

Following their parents' advice to be a positive influence, the brothers now challenge teens to do the same. Kevin, Joe and Nick

---

好榜样

不检行为是时下许多名人的正字标记，"强纳斯兄弟"可谓一股清流。他们不但不抽烟、喝酒和嗑药，反而会一起祷告、戴贞洁戒和打高尔夫球！

青少年歌迷喜欢他们愉快的歌曲，家长则欣赏他们意涵纯正的歌词和积极正面的讯息，这些要素使得"强纳斯兄弟"跻身最受欢迎的热门摇滚乐团之列。

为善不落人后

强纳斯兄弟听从父母要求他们发挥正面影响的建议，现在也激励青少

---

purity *n.* 纯洁
wholesome *adj.* 有良好道德影响的

upbeat *adj.* 乐观的；快乐的
ingredient *n.* 要素；因素

established "Change for the Children" as a way for kids to help less-fortunate children. Through this *foundation*, people can choose one of five different charities and *donate* to it. Kids are encouraged to give their own money, or if they borrow from their parents, to pay it back. And for the first $10,000 given to each charity, the Jonas Brothers promise to match it.

For Nick Jonas, one of the charities the band selected has a special *significance*.

American Diabetes Association

In 2005, Nick began losing weight very quickly, experiencing *frequent* thirst and making frequent trips to the bathroom. A hospital

---

年起而效尤。凯文、乔和尼克成立了"为孩童作出改变"基金会，让孩子们得以向弱势孩童伸出援手。通过这个基金会，民众可以在五个慈善机构中任选一个捐出善款，他们鼓励小朋友捐出自己的钱，或假如他们向爸妈借钱，也要还钱，并承诺在每个机构首度募集10,000元善款后，也捐出同等金额。

对尼克·强纳斯而言，乐团所选的其中一个慈善机构具有特殊意义。

美国糖尿病协会

2005年，尼克的体重开始迅速下滑，经常觉得口渴，也常上洗手间。他去医院检查后，发现自己得了糖尿病。将近四年后，尼克学会如何

---

foundation *n.* 基金会
significance *n.* 重要性；意义

donate *v.* 捐赠
frequent *adj.* 频繁的

checkup revealed that he had diabetes. Almost four years later, Nick has learned how to manage his disease. In fact, he *maintains* a busy schedule and full life in spite of it. He speaks about it openly at many of his concerts and encourages other young people with diabetes. Through their foundation, the band hopes to raise *awareness* of diabetes and money for the American Diabetes Association.

Family ties

Whenever the brothers are asked what makes them so successful, they always *credit* their close-knit family. Their father, mother and younger brother all travel with them. According to the

---

与疾病共舞，事实上，尽管他身患糖尿病，还是行程满档，生活充实。他常在他的演唱会上公开提及病史，鼓励了其他年轻的病友，通过他们的基金会，这个乐团希望能提高民众对糖尿病的认识，也能为"美国糖尿病协会"募款。

亲情力量

每当有人问起三兄弟成功的关键，他们一定归功于家人间亲密的情感。他们的父亲、母亲和小弟都跟着他们四处旅行，三兄弟说，父母一直

---

maintain *v.* 保持；维持　　　　　　　　　awareness *n.* 意识
credit *v.* 把……归于；归功于

brothers, their parents have always supported them and today help to keep them *humble*.

What's ahead?

With lots of projects *lined up*, it looks like the sky's limit for the band. One thing's for sure, the Jonas Brothers are certainly "living the dream" while doing what they do best – performing together!

为他们加油打气，如今更努力让他们不要恃宠而骄。

未来的打算？

这个乐团还有好多案子等着他们，看来前途真是不可限量，有一点毋庸置疑，"强纳斯兄弟"做的是他们最擅长的事，就是一起表演，可说是"梦想起飞"的写照！

humble *adj.* 谦虚的；谦逊的　　　　　line up 组织；安排

24

Cathy Freeman

Introduction

The whole world watched a *determined* young woman win the gold in the 400-meter *dash* at the 2000 Olympic Games in Sydney, Australia. Her name is Cathy Freeman. She is an *Aborigine* — one of a group of people who are native to Australia. She accepted the medal for her country, Australia, and for her people, the Aborigine. She was the first Aborigine to capture such a

凯西·弗里曼

简介

2000年悉尼奥运会400米金牌争夺战中，全世界目睹了一位坚毅的年轻女子赢得了这枚宝贵的金牌。她叫凯西·弗里曼。她是土著人——澳洲土著居民的一部分。这枚金牌，为她的国家——澳大利亚，也为她的同胞——土著民，而赢。她是第一位获此殊荣的土著运动员。她是土著居民强有力的希望象征。她也是世界人民走向更加互相理解的强有

---

determined *adj.* 坚定的
Aborigine *n.* 澳大利亚土著

dash *n.* 短跑

high honor. She is a powerful symbol of the hopes of the Aboriginal people. She is also a powerful symbol for more understanding among people all over the world.

Aboriginal and Australian Past

The Aborigine (ab-uh-RIJ-uh-nee) are the first people who lived in Australia, before Europeans settled there. The word "Aborigine" means "from the beginning" and refers to the *indigenous*, or original people of Australia. They *roamed* the country both in the milder coastal regions and in the *harsh* interior desert lands, called the "outback." They are a dark-skinned people, grouped into *tribes*, with their own spiritual beliefs and ways of living.

English explorers under Captain James Cook claimed Australia as a colony for Great Britain in 1780. British settlers soon followed. They believed their way of life was better than the tribal ways and

---

力的象征。

土著民和澳大利亚的历史

土著民（ab-uh-RIJ）是欧洲移民定居在澳大利亚之前，最先生活在这里的居民。"土著"就是"从一开始"的意思，指的就是最原始的，或最初的澳大利亚居民。他们游荡在气候温和的沿海地区，也游走于环境恶劣的沙漠地区，被叫做"内地"。他们属于深色皮肤人种，群居于部落，有着自己的精神信仰和生活方式。

1780年，英国探险家们在詹姆斯·库克船长的带领下，宣布澳大利亚为大英帝国的一个殖民地。不久，英国移民定居于此。他们认为自己的

---

indigenous *adj.* 本地的；当地的
harsh *adj.* 恶劣的；艰苦的

roam *v.* 闲逛；漫步
tribe *n.* 部落

called the Aborigines *inferior*. There was a great deal of fighting between the newcomers and the Aborigines. The British newcomers had much more powerful weapons and were able to *defeat* the Aborigines.

The fighting was often very cruel, and large numbers of Aborigines were killed. The British set up a new government based on the British way of life. They ruled the whole country and forced their own religion, *Christianity*, on the Aboriginal people.

The new rulers looked upon the Aborigines as *savages* and gave them no rights. Aborigines were forced to live separately from the settlers. Most of the Aborigines lived in the remote outback, often

---

生活方式优于土著居民，称他们为劣等居民。英国移民与澳大利亚土著民之间发生了许多斗争。英国新进移民的武器相比之下更有力，足以打败土著民。

斗争通常是残酷的，大量土著民被杀。英国移民基于自己的生活方式成立了新政府。他们统治着整个国家，强迫土著居民接受他们的宗教——基督教。

新统治者们视土著民为野蛮人群，不赋予他们任何权利。土著民被迫与他们分隔而居。绝大多数的土著民生活在偏远的内地，通常被安置在居

---

inferior *n.* 级别低的人
Christianity *n.* 基督教

defeat *v.* 打败；战胜
savage *n.* 野蛮人

placed on *reservations* or church *missions*. Some lived on the outskirts of towns where they worked for the Europeans for little or no pay. The government tried to force European ways on the Aboriginal people and destroy their languages and their ways of living and believing.

Over 200 years ago when the English first settled in Australia, there were between one million and three million Aborigines speaking about 250 different languages. Now there are only about 200,000 (45,000 full-blood), speaking only 100 languages. They have *died off* in very large numbers during the past 200 years. They have died because of terrible fighting, diseases brought by the Europeans, and poor living conditions.

留地或履行宗教任务。也有一些土著民生活在市郊，为那些欧洲移民提供服务，但也只能得到极其微薄的收入或分文不入。当地政府努力将欧洲的生活方式强加于土著民，试图摧毁他们的语言、生活方式和信仰。

200多年前，当英国人最初定居在澳大利亚的时候，土著居民有100万到300万，讲着大约250种不同的语言。而如今，只剩下大约20万（45,000为纯血统）土著居民讲着100种不同的语言。在过去的200年间，他们大批消失，或死于残酷的斗争，或死于欧洲人带来的疾病，或死于恶劣的生活环境。

---

reservation *n.* 保留地；居留地   mission *n.* 任务
die off 消失

Even as recently as 1951, the Australian government passed laws that did not allow Aborigines to own property. They were not allowed to take certain jobs, to marry whom they wanted, to move where they wanted, or to live by their own ways.

Cathy's Early Years

Catherine Astrid Salome Freeman was born to Aboriginal parents on February 16, 1973. She grew up in a small town on the east coast of Australia with her immediate family and many *cousins*. Cathy's grandfather, known as "The King," was an outstanding football player and an *excellent* runner. Her father, Norman Freeman, also a fine athlete, *upheld* the family's reputation on the football field. Cathy was fortunate to have *inherited* her athletic talent from both of these men.

甚至在最近的1951年，澳洲政府通过了禁止土著居民拥有财产的法律。禁止他们从事某些工作，不得随意结婚，不得随意流动，或按自己的意愿生活。

凯西的早年

1973年2月16日，凯西·弗里曼出生在一个土著家庭。她和直系亲属生活在澳大利亚东海岸的一个小镇，与许多堂兄妹一起长大。凯西的祖父，被叫做"部落长"，是个出色的足球运动员和优秀的田径运动员。她的父亲，诺曼·弗里曼，也是一位杰出的运动员，在足球领域维护着家族的荣誉。凯西非常幸运地继承了两位前辈的运动天赋。

---

cousin *n.* 堂只弟姐妹
uphold *v.* 维护

excellent *adj.* 卓越的；杰出的
inherit *v.* 继承

Cathy's mother, Cecelia, was half Aborigine. She had been raised on *Palm* Island, off the Queensland coast. Cecelia's mother (Cathy's beloved grandmother Nanna Sibley) and her relatives were removed from their tribal home to Palm Island. This was part of the government's rulings to move Aborigines away from their original land. This kind of unjust treatment in her own family helped Cathy to develop a fighting spirit.

When Cathy was five years old, her father left the family after being very sick and developing a drinking problem. Cathy's mother *struggled* to earn a living to support her family. Her second daughter, Anne Marie, had been born with a *disabling* illness. At nine years of age, Anne Marie had been placed in a home for children with special needs. To Cathy, her sister's disability reminded her of how fortunate she was to have a healthy, strong body with which to *accomplish* her

---

　　凯西的母亲，塞塞莉娅，有一半的土著血统。她在昆士兰岛海岸附近的棕榈岛长大。塞塞莉娅的母亲（凯西深爱的外祖母希波利）及亲属被从部落据点驱逐。让土著民远离他们原始的土地这是政府统治土著居民政策的一部分。家族遭遇的不公平待遇帮助凯西培养了一种战斗精神。

　　当凯西5岁时，父亲得了一场大病，并养成了酗酒恶习，之后便离开了家。凯西的母亲努力挣钱养家。家中的第二个女儿，安·玛利亚天生残疾。在9岁时，妹妹被送到了儿童福利院。对凯西而言，妹妹的不幸时刻提醒着自己是多么的幸运，拥有一个健康的、强壮的身体，能让她实现她

---

palm *n.* 棕榈
disable *v.* 使丧失能力；使伤残

struggle *v.* 奋斗；努力
accomplish *v.* 完成

dreams.

Cathy ran her first race when she was six. Her teachers and her new stepfather, Bruce Barber, recognized her speed, grace, and energy as she ran *laps* around the local track. Bruce *predicted* that she would become an Olympic star, and he set about to help make it happen. Cathy started her training with the dream that she would some day become a champion Olympic runner.

At age eleven, Cathy set a new national record in the high jump at a big track meet in Melbourne. In the same year, she won state titles in the 100-meter and 200-meter *sprints* and the high jump for her age group.

Encouraged by her family, Cathy attended excellent high school

---

的梦想。

6岁时，凯西参加了她的第一场比赛。当她绕着赛道奔跑时，她的老师和继父布鲁斯·巴伯，注意到了她所迸发出的速度，体现出的优雅和爆发出的力量。布鲁斯预测，凯西将成为一名奥运新星，并开始着手让这成为现实。为了有一天能实现奥运冠军的梦想，凯西开始投入到了训练中。

11岁那年，在墨尔本田径运动会的跳高比赛中，凯西创下了新的全国纪录。同年，在年龄组的100米和200米短距离赛跑及跳高比赛中，获得州冠军。

在家人的鼓励下，凯西带着奖学金进入了重点高中。经专业教练的

---

lap *n.* （跑道等的）一圈   predict *v.* 预测
sprint *n.* 短跑比赛

on *scholarships*. She trained under a professional coach who prepared her for her first great victory when she was sixteen. She won a gold medal in the 4 x 100-meter *relay* team at the Commonwealth Games in 1990. That same year, she was voted Young Australian of the Year. In the following year, she was named Aboriginal Athlete of the Year.

The Aborigines Win Some Rights

During the decade of the 1960s, Cathy's tribal people were speaking out to gain more rights. The first important success was a law passed in 1967 that allowed Aborigines to become citizens. This law gave them the right to vote and to receive some government benefits. They were finally able to have a say in Australian government policies.

培训，凯西正为她第一次大的胜利蓄势待发。那年，她16岁。1990年，英联邦国家运动会上，凯西在4 x 100接力赛中摘得金牌。同年，被授予该年度"澳大利亚杰出青年奖"。次年，又获得该年度"最佳土著运动员奖"。

土著民争取权利

20世纪60年代的10年间，凯西的部落族人正大胆地行动以争取更多的权利。首要成功的事件便是1967年通过了承认土著居民公民身份的法律。这条法律赋予了土著居民选举和接受一些政府福利的权利。他们终于在澳大利亚政府政策的制定中有了发言权。

---

scholarship *n.* 奖学金　　　　　　　relay *n.* 接力赛

The Aborigines also *spoke out* to protect their lands. Their belief, similar to Native Americans in the United States and Canada, is that the land is *sacred* and cannot be owned by individuals. They worked to protect their land from development and from use by non-Aborigines who would not treat it with respect. They also worked for the right to have their own government instead of being *governed* by European laws that did not respect their ways. In 1972, a law was passed that gave the Aborigines some of the rights they demanded.

Cathy on the Road to Success

These gains in citizenship and the right to own and manage land were great victories for the Aborigines. They have had more than 200 years of *mistreatment* to overcome. Cathy Freeman was becoming

---

此外，土著居民还勇敢地行动起来保护他们的领地。与美国加拿大的印第安土著相似，他们相信，这片土地是神圣的，是不能被个人占有的。他们联合起来，保护他们的领地不受非土著居民的亵渎、开发和滥用。他们也努力争取拥有自己政府的权利，而不是受治于不会尊重他们自己生活方式的欧洲法律。1972年，通过了一条法律，允许土著民拥有一些他们主张的权利。

凯西的成功之路

对土著居民而言，公民身份的被认可和拥有并管理自己领地权利的取得，是巨大的胜利。他们为此克服了200多年不公的待遇。凯西·弗里曼因其超凡的运动天赋而知名度大增，但是身为土著民，她仍要克服许多来

---

speak out 挺身；公开站出来　　　　　　sacred *adj.* 神圣的
govern *v.* 统治；管理　　　　　　　　mistreatment *n.* 虐待

widely known for her *amazing* running ability, but as an Aborigine she still had to deal with many non-Aborigines thinking she was inferior.

Cathy took great pride in who she was and wanted all the people in Australia to be proud of her *accomplishments*, both as an Aborigine and as an Australian. She tried to speak out to correct the wrongs against her people. It wasn't always easy, but she had courage and determination.

In 1994, at the Commonwealth Games in Victoria, British columbia Canada Cathy won gold medals in the 200-meter and 400-meter races. In celebration, she ran around the track carrying both the red-white-and-blue Australian flag and the black-red-and-

---

自非土著民的偏见和歧视。

凯西以她身为土著民而骄傲，她要让全澳大利亚人都为她的成就感到骄傲，不仅是作为土著民，而且是作为澳大利亚人。她努力着，勇敢地去更正土著同胞们所遭受的不公。然而，这并非易事，但她从没丧失勇气和毅力。

1994年，在加拿大不列颠哥伦比亚省的维多利亚市举行的英联邦运动会上，凯西摘得200米和400米比赛的金牌。在庆祝的时刻，凯西绕着跑道，同时举起红白蓝的澳大利亚国旗和黑红黄的土著旗。一些人对她展示土著旗帜这一举动并不赞同。他们认为凯西的所作所为是一种抗议。凯

---

amazing *adj.* 惊人的　　　　　　accomplishment *n.* 成就

yellow Aboriginal flag. Some people *disapproved* of her showing the tribal flag. They said what she did was an act of protest. Cathy responded that she was merely showing her national pride. After some time, it became clear that all the people of Australia, both non-Aboriginal and Aboriginal, were looking upon this young, *remarkable*, world-class runner as a real champion. She was winning the support of all people in her rise to fame.

Cathy's dream of going to the Olympic Games came true in 1996 at Atlanta, Georgia. She ran the 400-meter *dash* in her best time ever. It made her the sixth fastest woman in history, but she lost the gold medal to an even faster runner. She did win the silver, and with it, the respect and admiration of the Australian people.

西回应道，她只是在表达她的民族骄傲感。没多久，不仅是土著同胞，还有非土著居民都一致赞同，这个年轻的、超凡的、世界级的运动员是真正的冠军。随着她的名字家喻户晓，凯西获得了所有人的支持。

1996年，凯西参加奥运会的梦想实现了。在400米的比赛中，她取得了她有史以来最好的成绩。这使得她成为历史上跑得最快的女人，但是她与金牌失之交臂了，她赢得了银牌，也赢得了澳大利亚人的尊敬和钦佩。

---

disapprove *v.* 不赞成
dash *n.* 短跑

remarkable *adj.* 非凡的

The following year, she won a major international track title at a World Championship event in Athens, Greece. As she circled the *stadium* in the victory lap, she again carried both the Australian and Aboriginal flags, and no one objected. Soon after, she was named Australian of the Year. This took her another step toward being an important role model for Aborigines. In doing so, she was helping all Australians come together as one people.

The years 1998 and 1999 brought Cathy even more success. She again won the 400-meter title at a World Championship event and the national title at Melbourne. She showed her great belief in herself and in her ability to succeed through *constant* training. She would not

---

1997年，在希腊雅典举行的世界锦标赛上，凯西获得国际田径赛冠军。当她再次手持澳大利亚国旗和土著旗绕道庆祝时，没人发出质疑。不久，她当选了当年的"澳大利亚年度人物"。这使她作为土著民的重要模范的角色又大大提升了一步。与此同时，她也是在帮助所有的澳大利亚人作为一个民族团结起来。

1998年和1999年里，凯西收获了更多的成功。在墨尔本举行的世界锦标赛和全国锦标赛上，凯西再次摘得400米桂冠。通过不断的训练，凯西坚定了自己能够取得成功的信念和能力。但她并没有被胜利冲昏头脑。她说，"金钱可以使生活变得容易，但是我不想成为富人……，也不想成

---

stadium *n.* 体育馆   constant *adj.* 持续的

let success go to her head. Cathy said, "Money makes life easier but I don't want to be rich... I don't want to be a celebrity either... As long as my family and loved ones are there, I'm happy... My family has always come first. I have always found security and comfort in their arms."

Olympic Fame

The Olympic Games of the Year 2000 were held in Sydney, Australia. Cathy Freeman was a leading *contender* for a gold medal. She was honored by being chosen to light the Olympic torch. Then, in a *stunning* 400-meter run, Cathy won Australia's 100th gold medal

---

为名人……只要有家人的陪伴，我就是幸福的……我的家人永远都是第一位的。在家人的怀抱里，我始终都能感到安全和舒适。"

奥运名气

2000年奥运会在澳大利亚首都悉尼举行。凯西·弗雷曼是主要的金牌角逐者。她非常荣耀地被推选来点燃奥运圣火。随后，在非常精彩的400米比赛中，凯西在自己国家的体育馆里为澳大利亚赢得了第100枚金

---

contender *n.* 角逐者；竞争者　　　　stunning *adj.* 绝妙的；极有魅力的

in a stadium in her own country. All Australians cheered wildly as they watched her carry both flags in her victory lap. Together they sang the national *anthem* and proudly spoke out "our Cathy." Cathy presented her *bouquet* of Australian flowers to her mother, Cecelia, whose teary face was filled with pride and joy.

Cathy Freeman is a real world champion, both on the running track and in life. She has become a role model for all Australians. She has shown the world that you can become what you want to be by working hard to reach your goals. And for the entire world, she has given hope for greater understanding among all people.

牌。当看到凯西在取得胜利的时刻手举两面旗帜，所有澳大利亚人欢呼雀跃。他们共同地唱起国歌，并骄傲地喊出"我们的凯西"。凯西把土著澳大利亚花束献给了母亲，塞塞莉娅。此时，母亲的脸上挂满了骄傲和喜悦的泪水。

凯西·弗里曼在比赛和生活中都是一位真正的世界冠军。她是所有澳大利亚人的榜样。她向世界展示通过努力，你可以实现自己的目标。她对于全世界人们之间能有更好的理解寄予了希望。

anthem *n.* 国歌

bouquet *n.* 花束

25

Mozart

The Toddler Pianist

Leopold Mozart walked into the *chapel* in Salzburg, Austria followed by his two small children.

"I'd like to sign my daughter Nannerl up for music lessons. She is eight years old, and I already believe she has quite a talent for music," he said to the organist. The organist, Anton, *smirked* a bit, for he knew how Leopold could *boast* about his children. "So, when will you be signing up the little boy?" Anton asked.

莫扎特

学步的儿童钢琴师

利奥波德·莫扎特走进了奥地利萨尔斯堡的教堂，后面跟着他的两个孩子。

"我要签字把女儿南内尔送来学习音乐课程，她现在是八岁，我相信她有良好的音乐天资，"他对风琴师说。这个风琴师叫做安东，傻笑了一下，他知道利奥波德是怎样吹自己的孩子的。"那么，你什么时候把你的小儿子送来学习呢？"安东问。

---

chapel *n.* 教堂
boast *v.* 自夸

smirk *v.* 傻笑

Leopold laughed at the joke, for little Wolfgang was only three years old. "Not for at least five years—I think eight is certainly young enough. Little Wolfgang's fingers would barely be able to *stretch* over the keys."

The organist promised to sign Nannerl up. Before Leopold left, the organist called Nannerl over to the church piano. "Come, I will give you a beginner lesson," he said. Nannerl ran over to her father, and Wolfgang *toddled* happily after her.

"Me too, Papa, me too!" he cried.

"No, no, Wolfgang, you are too small," said his father. "Pianos are not meant for little folks to touch, so please go outside and play."

利奥波德对这种玩笑大笑起来，小沃尔夫冈现在只有3岁。"不到5岁是不行的，我认为8岁就够小的了。小沃尔夫冈的手指张开还不能摸到琴键呢。"

风琴师答应收下南内尔。在利奥波德离开前，风琴师把南内尔叫到教堂的钢琴旁。"过来，我教你一个入门的课程吧，"他说。南内尔跑到她爸爸那里去了，沃尔夫冈兴高采烈地蹒跚到她的身后。

"我也是，爸爸我也是！"他叫喊着。

"不，不行，沃尔夫冈，你太小了，"爸爸说，"钢琴不是给小家伙们摸的，所以请你到外面去玩吧。"

---

stretch *v.* 伸开；伸展   toddle *v.* 蹒跚行走

Wolfgang turned around *obediently*. If his father had seen the *disappointed* look on little Wolfgang's face, it would have broken his heart. Wolfgang went outside and played near the door of the church, but his every thought was on the piano.

After Nannerl and Leopold had finished, they went to speak with the organist again. Wolfgang *crept* up to the piano and put his little hands on the keyboard. He began to play the simple *scales* he had heard his elder sister practicing.

The sound entranced him, and he played the scales over and over, playing them exactly right. He forgot everything else — he did not notice his father and sister standing behind him. He didn't even

---

　　沃尔夫冈听话地转了过去，如果爸爸看到沃尔夫冈脸上的失望，爸爸的心一定会碎的。沃尔夫冈到了外面，在教堂门附近玩去了，但他的心还在钢琴上。

　　南内尔和利奥波德完成后，他们又过来和风琴师说话了。沃尔夫冈爬到了钢琴那里，把他的小手放在琴键上。他开始演奏他听到的姐姐练习的简单音程。

　　声音吸引着他，他一遍遍地演奏着这个音程，演得非常正确。他把别的东西都忘了，他没有注意到他的爸爸和姐姐就站在他的身后，他甚至没有听到他爸爸喊风琴师过来看。他把自己全部包裹在音乐之中了。他开始

---

obediently *adv.* 顺从地；服从地　　　　disappointed *adj.* 失望的

creep *v.* 爬　　　　　　　　　　　　　scale *n.* 音阶

hear his father shouting for the organist to come and see. He was completely *wrapped* up in the music. He began changing the scales, even inventing simple *tunes* of his own. Leopold stared at his young son Wolfgang. The boy was a musical *prodigy*.

The Child Wonder

Mozart played music as naturally as he breathed. When he was four years old, it took him only half an hour to learn a difficult piece of music that was written down. If he heard the piece, even if he heard it only once, he could *memorize* it instantly. When Wolfgang was five, Leopold and a friend came in to find him bending over a piece of paper and writing big, black notes, smearing and splattering ink everywhere.

"Wolfgang, what are you doing spoiling the nice, clean paper?" his father asked.

变换音程，甚至还发明了自己的简单曲调。利奥波德瞪圆了眼睛看着这小儿子沃尔夫冈，他是音乐天才。

孩子的奇迹

莫扎特把音乐演奏得像呼吸一样自然，在他4岁时，他只需要半小时就能学会一段很难的曲谱儿。如果他能听到一段曲子，甚至只听一遍，他就能马上记住，沃尔夫冈5岁时，利奥波德和朋友进来时，发现他俯身在一张纸上，正在写一大大的、黑色的音符，把墨汁溅洒得到处都是。

"沃尔夫冈，你把这样一张漂亮而干净的纸搞成这样是做什么呢？"他的爸爸问。

---

wrap *v.* 包；裹
prodigy *n.* 天才

tune *n.* 曲调；曲子
memorize *v.* 记住

"Papa, I'm writing a *concerto*," Mozart said, his little eyes shining. His father picked up the paper and laughed. But soon his *amusement* turned to *amazement*. It was a concerto, composed of several instruments. He could see that the notes were correct, despite the smears and blotches.

"But Wolfgang, this music would be too difficult for anyone to play," he said.

"Oh, no, it would only take some practice. See, it goes like this," said Wolfgang, and he ran to the piano. He placed his *smudged* paper on the music stand and began to play.

His father's friend had been laughing — he'd assumed Leopold was just playing along with Wolfgang. But now he saw that the child was a true wonder.

"爸爸，我在写交响曲，"莫扎特说，他的小小眼睛闪着亮光。爸爸拿起来这张纸笑了，但没过多久他的高兴变成了惊奇，这的确是一个交响曲，由多个乐器组成。他发现所有的音符都是对的，虽然上面有涂抹和污渍。

"但是沃尔夫冈，你这个交响曲让任何人弹都是很难的，"爸爸说。

"哦，不，只需要练习一下就可以，看着，他是这样开始的，"沃尔夫冈说，他跑向钢琴，他把他弄脏的纸放在谱架上，开始演奏。

他爸爸的朋友一直在大笑，他认为利奥波德在和沃尔夫冈开玩笑。但现在他看到这个孩子就是奇迹。

---

concerto *n.* 协奏曲　　　　　　　　　amusement *n.* 愉悦；娱乐
amazement *n.* 惊奇　　　　　　　　　smudge *v.* 变模糊

"You ought to travel with him," the friend suggested. "He should be playing for *emperors*, for kings and queens."

"Perhaps I will," said his father.

The following year, when Wolfgang was only six years old, he and Nannerl started on tour. Wherever Wolfgang went to play, people would *giggle* at him. He was so small compared to the big piano, and his feet couldn't even touch the floor. But when he began to play, the audience fell silent. His playing was perfect and beautiful.

The first place they went to play was in Vienna, the capital of Austria. On the way, they stopped to visit a *monastery* in the little town of Ipo. There was a great *pipe organ* in the chapel.

"你应该带他旅行，"朋友建议说，"他应该给皇上、国王、国后演奏。"

"也许我会的，"他爸爸说。

第二年沃尔夫冈只有6岁，他和南内尔开始巡回演出。无论沃尔夫冈到哪里表演，人们都会把他逗笑，相对于大大钢琴来说，他是太小了。他的两条腿几乎够不到地面。但当他开始弹起来的时候，所有的听众一下子安静下来，他的演奏太完美了，太漂亮了。

他们去演奏的第一个地方是维也纳，这是奥地利的首都。在路上，他们停下来方问了衣普小镇的一个寺院，在小教堂里有一个很大的管风琴。

---

emperor *n.* 皇帝　　　　　　　　　giggle *v.* 咯咯地笑
monastery *n.* 寺院　　　　　　　　pipe organ 管风琴

"I want to play on it," Wolfgang said. "Papa, explain the *pedals* to me." Wolfgang's father helped his son onto the high stool. He was too small to even *operate* the pedals, so he walked across them instead. The music poured out of the chapel, growing more and more powerful. The *monks*, who had been at dinner, rushed into the room.

Because Wolfgang was so small, the monks could not see him, and they thought the organ was playing itself.

"It's an angel!" they cried. "Such music must come from heaven!"

Wolfgang was also very charming. Everywhere he went, people were *smitten* with this little musician. The customs officials asked him why he came to Vienna.

"我想演奏这个琴，"沃尔夫冈说，"爸爸告诉我这几个踏板怎样使用吧。"沃尔夫冈的爸爸帮助儿子坐在凳子上。他太小了，几乎无法操作踏板，所以就像在这些踏板上奔跑一样。音乐从教堂飘出来，变得越来越有魔力，道士们正在吃饭，都跑到了房间里。

因为沃尔夫冈太小了，道士们看不到他，他们认为是风琴自己在演奏。

"那是一个天使，"他们大喊着，"这样的音乐一定是来自天堂。"

沃尔夫冈还非常可爱，无论到了哪里，人们都会被这个小音乐家迷住的。海关人员问他为什么到维也纳。

---

pedal *n.* 踏板　　　　　　　　　operate *v.* 操作
monk *n.* 僧侣；修道士　　　　　smitten *adj.* 突然爱上的

"I come to play the piano," he said.

"Why, you're no bigger than a chicken. You can't be old enough to play anything but a *whistle*."

"I'll show you," Wolfgang said. He asked the officials to open the box containing his piano, and the little boy began to play right in the customs house. A crowd gathered around in *awe*. The head of customs immediately gave the order to let the Mozart family through without difficulty.

After playing in Vienna, Wolfgang was invited to spend the day with the royal children. One of the princesses was the famous Marie Antoinette, who was just a little girl about Wolfgang's age.

Wolfgang liked her very much. She took him around the *palace*

"我是来演奏钢琴的，"他说。

"是吗？你还没有一只鸡大，你除了能演奏口哨外，你还没能大到演奏别的东西。"

"我给你看看，"沃尔夫冈说，他请官员打开他装钢琴的箱子，这个小家伙在海关开始表演。一大群人挤在这里惊喜地看着，海关的主管马上下令让莫扎特全家顺利过关。

在维也纳表演结束后，沃尔夫冈被邀请和皇家的孩子一起过几天。有一个公主是有名的玛丽·安托瓦内特，与沃尔夫冈正好是同龄。

沃尔夫冈非常喜欢她，她带他在宫廷里转来转去，让他看所有神奇的

---

whistle *n.* 哨子；口哨

palace *n.* 宫殿

awe *n.* 敬畏；惊叹

to show him all the wonderful riches. He was not used to such smoothly *polished* floors, and he *slipped* and fell. All the children laughed except Marie. After she helped him up, Wolfgang said, "When I am a man, I will marry you."

The princess's servant *gasped*. Then Wolfgang put his arms around Marie and gave her a big kiss. "*Dreadful*!" cried the servant, for it was never, ever allowed for a common person to touch royalty. But Marie only laughed, took Wolfgang's hand, and gave him a kiss back.

The Poor Young Man

Wolfgang, his father, and his sister toured all around Europe. Wolfgang's fame grew, and he became a very handsome young man.

富人们。他不习惯这样抛光的地板，他滑倒了。所有的孩子都笑了，只有玛丽没有笑。她把他扶起来以后，沃尔夫冈说，"等我长大了，我会来娶你的。"

公主的仆人大吸一口凉气，然后沃尔夫冈抱住玛丽，轻轻地亲了她一下。"太可恶了！"仆人叫道，因为永远、绝对是不能让平民触碰皇家的。但是玛丽只是笑了一下，拉着沃尔夫冈的手，也亲了他一下。

可怜的年轻人

沃尔夫冈、他的爸爸和姐姐在整个欧洲巡回。沃尔夫冈的名声越来越大，而且长成一个非常潇洒的小伙子。但遗憾的是，音乐家的生活收入并

---

polished *adj.* 抛光的

gasp *v.* 倒抽气；喘气

slip *v.* 滑倒

dreadful *adj.* 讨厌的

But unfortunately, the life of a musician did not pay well. People were less impressed with his playing as he got older. After all, a six-year-old musician was a *marvel*, but a twenty-year-old musician was nothing new.

For his entire adult life, Wolfgang Mozart was very poor. Once, a friend came to visit him and found Wolfgang and his young wife *waltzing* around their apartment. They were not dancing for joy; they were dancing to try and keep warm, because they could not *afford* fuel.

Wolfgang's wife, Constance, was often ill. They also had little children to take care of. Everyone agreed that his music was wonderful, but writing, selling, and playing music did not bring in

---

不是很好。随着他年龄的增长，人们对他的表演的兴趣变小了。无论怎样讲，6岁的音乐家是一个神奇，但是20岁的音乐家就没有什么新意了。

沃尔夫冈·莫扎特的整个一生中都是很穷的，有一次，他的一个朋友来看他，发现沃尔夫冈和他的妻子在自己的公寓中跳着华尔兹，他们不是为了取乐而跳的，他们是为了取暖而跳的，因为他们付不起燃料的费用。

沃尔夫冈的妻子，康斯坦丝，总好生病，他们还有小孩子需要照顾。所有的人都认为他的音乐是神奇的，但是靠创作、出卖和演奏音乐换不来多少钱。

---

marvel *n.* 奇迹   waltz *v.* 跳华尔兹舞
afford *v.* 买得起

much money.

The Requiem

One day when Mozart was thirty-six, a tall stranger dressed in gray pounded on his door. Without saying a word, he handed Mozart an *envelope*. Inside was some money and an order for Mozart to write a requiem. Nothing in the envelope said whom it was for.

"It is for myself," Mozart said to Constance. "I feel it in my heart."

She laughed. He was only thirty-six, and it was silly for him to talk of dying!

The truth was that the requiem had been ordered by a *count*. He wanted to play the music at his wife's *funeral*, but he wanted to say that he had written it himself. But Mozart didn't know this.

安魂弥撒曲

莫扎特36岁时有一天，一个高个子穿着灰色衣服的陌生人重重地敲着他的门。一句话没有说就递给了莫扎特一个信封，里面是一些钱和请莫扎特写一个安魂弥撒曲的订单。里面没有说是为谁写的。

"这是为我自己写的，"莫扎特对康斯坦丝说，"我在内心中都能感受到。"

她笑了，他只有36岁，说到死亡真是有些荒谬。

事实上，这个安魂弥撒曲是一个伯爵订购的，他想在他妻子的葬礼上演奏这首曲子，但他想说这首曲子是他自己写的，但是莫扎特不知道这些。

---

envelope *n.* 信封
funeral *n.* 葬礼

count *n.* 伯爵

Wolfgang began writing. He wrote *feverishly*, staying up all night, sometimes even forgetting to eat. The work *exhausted* him, and he began to grow weak. Mozart had been making a little money by teaching music students. But now he was so wrapped up in the requiem that he *cancelled* all of his classes.

Without money, the family couldn't afford much food. They couldn't afford candles to light their cold house at night. But still Mozart wrote, growing weaker and weaker. Finally, just before finishing the requiem, Mozart died. It truly had been his own requiem.

The Greatest Musician Who Ever Lived

Mozart is still considered the greatest musician who ever lived.

沃尔夫冈开始创作，他狂热地写着，晚上不睡，有时甚至忘记了吃饭。工作耗尽他的精力，他变得虚弱起来。莫扎特通过教学生能挣到一点钱，但是他现在是全身心地投入到安魂弥撒曲中，他取消了他所有的课程。

没有钱，家里买不起食物，他们买不起蜡烛来照亮晚上寒冷的房子。但是莫扎特仍就是写，身体越来越弱。最后刚好完成安魂弥撒曲时，莫扎特死了，这真是给他自己写的安魂弥撒曲。

有史以来最伟大的音乐家

莫扎特现在仍被认为是有史以来最伟大的音乐家，但是在他死的时

---

feverishly *adv.* 狂热地   exhaust *v.* （使）筋疲力尽
cancel *v.* 取消

But when he died, his family was so poor that they could not *purchase* a *gravestone*. Eventually, no one could remember where he had been buried. Today there is a great *monument* to Mozart in Vienna, and on it is an inscription reading, "The probable site of his grave."

Mozart's music is used everywhere. You can hear it in a concert hall, or you can hear it in cartoons. He wrote many of his most famous pieces when he was only a little older than you are. And he died while he was still young. Imagine the wealth of music we might have if he had only lived.

候，他家里太穷了，他们买不起一块墓碑，后来没有人能记住把他埋在哪里了。今天在维也纳有一个很大的莫扎特纪念碑，上面刻着"这里可能是他的坟墓。"

莫扎特的音乐应用广泛，你可以在交响大厅中听到，你可以在动画片中听到。他在比你年龄还小的时候就写出了很多有名的曲子。他年纪很轻时就去世了，可以想象，如果他能活着，我们该有什么样的音乐财富呢。

---

purchase *v.* 购买   gravestone *n.* 墓碑
monument *n.* 纪念碑

26

Vincent's Bedroom

Introduction

In 1888, an artist named Vincent Van Gogh moved from the Netherlands to Arles, France. Vincent was drawn to the beauty and calm of Arles. He liked the way the light from the night stars *glittered* across the Rhone River and the way the sunlight *glistened* over the yellow wheat that grew on the rolling hills.

文森特的卧室

引言

1888年，一位叫文森特·梵高的艺术家从荷兰搬到了法国的阿里斯，文森特是被阿里斯的美丽和宁静吸引到这里的，他喜欢夜空中的星光在罗纳河的天空中闪烁，他喜欢阳光在山坡黄色的麦田上闪亮。

---

glitter *v.* 闪亮；闪烁   glisten *v.* 闪光；闪亮

Vincent spent most of his days outside, painting pictures of the fields, sky, and sunflowers. This was a new way to paint in the mid-1800s, as most artists up to that point had always painted inside a *studio*.

Painting Emotions

Vincent was a man of many strong feelings. At times he felt sadder, angrier, or happier than other people. As his mind and his body *churned* with despair and delight, the emotions he felt led him to create some of his greatest paintings. He used his own style of putting color on the *canvas* with a brush to show his feelings.

文森特的大部分时间都是在户外度过的，他在画田野、天空和向日葵。这在18世纪中期还是属于一种新的画法，此前的艺术家总是在画室里作画。

绘画的情感

文森特的情感是很强烈的，有时他比其他人更悲伤、更愤怒、更高兴。由于他的头脑和身体随着他的失望和欢乐旋转，他所体会到的情感引领他创造出他最伟大的绘画。他用画笔在画布上涂色的方式表达自己的感情。

---

studio *n.* （艺术家的）工作室
canvas *n.* （帆布）画布

churn *v.* （使）猛烈翻腾

One of his most famous paintings is called Starry Night. In Vincent's mind, the night sky above Arles *swirled* with emotion. The sky felt alive to him, and he was able to capture its energy in his painting. He painted the moon and bright yellow stars twirling in a navy blue sky.

Because Vincent's moods changed often, he understood that he needed a calm and cheerful place in which to live and work. So he rented a bright yellow house and created a bedroom that would help him feel safe and calm.

他的一幅最有名的画叫做"星空",在文森特的头脑中,阿里斯的夜空是带有情绪地旋转的,天空对他来说是有生命的,而且他在他的画中是可以捕捉到能量。他画的月亮和明亮的黄色的星星在海蓝色的天空中是旋转的。

因为文森特的情绪经常变化,他明白自己需要在一个宁静和欢快的环境中生活和工作,所以他租了一个亮黄色的房子,建了一个能够帮助他感到安全和宁静的卧室。

---

swirl *n.* (使)打旋;旋动

A Comfortable Bedroom

In a letter written in October 1888 to his brother Theo, Vincent described his bedroom.

Well, I have painted the walls pale *violet*. The ground with checked material. The *wooden* bed and the chairs, yellow like butter; the sheet and the pillows lemon light green. The bedspread, *scarlet* coloured. The window green. The washbasin, orangey.

It was a good time for Vincent. In the mornings, he painted all

---

一个令人舒适的卧室

在1888年10月写给弟弟特奥的信中，文森特是这样描绘自己的卧室的：

好吧，我把墙涂成淡粉色，地面是有格子的。床和椅子都是木头的，和奶油一样的绿色，床单和枕头都是柠檬淡黄色。床罩是鲜红色的，窗户是绿色的，洗脸盆是黄色的（橘黄色）。

这是文森特最好的时光。上午他画各种各样的画，晚上他坐在房外的

---

violet *n.* 蓝紫色；紫罗兰色

scarlet *adj.* 鲜红的

wooden *adj.* 木制的

kinds of paintings. In the evenings, he sat in outdoor cafes and chatted with the people of Arles. Later in the evening, he enjoyed coming home to his comfortable bedroom.

The Bedroom Series

During the years 1888 and 1889, Vincent created five works of art showing his bedroom in Arles. Three were brightly colored oil paintings, and two were *sketches*. The three oil paintings, sometimes called the "Bedroom" series, show us a bit of what Vincent's life was like during the time when he painted the pictures.

咖啡馆里，与阿里斯的人聊天，再晚一些，他喜欢回到家里舒适的卧室。

卧室系列

1888至1889年间，文森特画了五幅他在阿里斯的卧室的画，其中三幅是亮色调的油画，其他两幅是素描。前三幅油画有时也叫做"卧室"系列，让我们了解一些他画这些画时的生活情况。

---

sketch *n.* 素描

Vincent was very close to his brother Theo. Theo supported Vincent's life as a painter. Vincent wrote many letters to Theo explaining his paintings and telling him about his life in Arles. Theo saved the letters, and today 847 of them can be seen and read in an online museum. In one of these letters, Vincent wrote about his bedroom and included a sketch.

My eyes are still tired by then I had a new idea in my head and here is the sketch of it.

文森特和他的弟弟特奥的关系很近，特奥给文森特作为画家的生活费用。文森特写给特奥很多的信件说明他的绘画，也告诉他在阿里斯的生活。特奥把这些信都留了下来，现在网上博物馆有847封信。其中的一封信中，文森特介绍了自己的房间，还有一个素描。

那里我的眼睛很累了，我脑袋里有了一个新的想法，这里的有一幅素描。

Vincent created a bedroom that was a simple, restful, cheery *haven*. His oil paintings show some of what life was like in 1888. Indoor plumbing didn't exist then, so if you look carefully at the paintings, you can see that Vincent kept water in his room for washing. He hung his clothes on *hooks*. Radios, televisions, and CD players had not been invented. Look at the painting. What do you think Vincent did for fun?

　　文森特把自己的卧室弄成简单、很休闲、很愉悦的避风港。他的油画也展示了1888年的生活。屋内当时还没有管道，所以如果你仔细看看油画，你可以看到文森特在室内有给自己洗漱用的水。他把衣服挂在钩子上。收音机、电视机和CP机当时都没有发明。看一下这幅画，你想想他用什么消遣呢？

---

haven *n.* 保护区；安全的地方　　　　　　　　　　hook *n.* 钩子

Similar and Different

Vincent painted for fun. He created more than 2,000 works of art during his lifetime. In Arles, he painted many *landscapes* and *portraits*. Each time he painted a picture of his bedroom, he included newer paintings he hung on his walls. Look at the pictures hanging on the walls. How do the pictures on the bedroom walls change from painting to painting?

Study the three paintings. In many ways they are similar, but some of the details are very different. Can you name three ways in which the paintings *differ*?

相同与差别

文森特为了消遣而画画，他的一生画了2000多幅画。在阿里斯他画了很多的风景和肖像。每次他画自己的卧室时，墙上都挂着一幅新的画。看一下墙上挂着的新画。卧室里墙上的每幅画都是变化的？

研究一下这三幅画，在很多方面，他们都是相似的，但只有一个细节是非常不同的，你能找到三种不同的地方吗？

---

landscape *n.* 风景
differ *v.* 不同

portrait *n.* 肖像

Vincent painted the first painting in October 1888. The painting was damaged when the Rhone River flooded the yellow house. His brother Theo really liked the painting and encouraged Vincent to create another painting to replace the damaged one. Vincent created the second painting in September 1889. Look at the two paintings. How do the paintings *express* what Vincent was feeling?

文森特画第一幅画时是1888年的10月，罗纳河的洪水淹了那所黄房子，所以把这幅图破坏了。特奥非常喜欢这幅图，他鼓励文森特再画一幅，把破坏的这个补上。文森特于1889年9月画了第二幅。看一下这两幅画，这两幅画是怎样表达文森特的感觉的？

express *v.* 表达

Where Can You See Vincent's Paintings?

Many people who like art agree that the only way to truly see a painting is to stand in front of it. However, to see just the few paintings in this book you would need to travel to America. However, the Internet created a way for people to see all of Vincent's works in one place. Visit www.vggallery.com to see how Vincent's painting style changed from his earliest works to his latest.

在哪里能看到文森特的画？

很多喜欢艺术的人都认为真正能看懂画的方法是站在画的前方。但是为了看到这本书中的几幅画，你需要到美国，但是网络会让人们在一个地方看到他所有的画。请访问www.vggallery.com看一下文森特从早期到最后的绘画风格变化。

In the summer of 1889, Vincent decided to make smaller *versions* of his favorite paintings. The painting of his bedroom was one of his favorites, so he painted a third version of it. This version was smaller than the other two versions. It was different in other ways as well. Look at the painting on the walls. How is it different from the paintings on pages 16 and 17?

Vincent's Style

To paint like Vincent, you would need to use:

1889年的夏天，文森特决定把他喜欢的画画成小一点儿的版本。卧室的画是他最喜欢的之一，所以他画第三个版本，这幅画比其他的要小一些，在其他方面也有一些不同。看看墙上的画，与16、17页上的画有什么不同。

文森特的风格

要想画成文森特那样，你需要使用：

---

version　*n.* 版本

- large swirls of color
- thick, short brush strokes
- colors that express feelings
- colors that nourish

Vincent Van Gogh loved color. He used color to express his feelings. He loved the colors of the sky, butter, wheat, and light from the sun. The colors he chose for his bedroom made him feel *content* and glad to be home.

- 旋转的颜色
- 粗而短的笔画
- 表达感情的颜色
- 消失的颜色

文森特·梵高喜欢颜色，他用颜色表达自己的感情。他喜欢天空的颜色、奶油的颜色、麦子的颜色，还喜欢太阳光。他为自己卧室选择的颜色让他感到很满足，让他喜欢回家。

---

content *adj.* 满足的

Think about how colors affect you. Do bright colors make you feel happy? Can dark colors make you feel sad? If this were your bedroom, what colors would you use to *decorate* it? Color this drawing to create a bedroom that would make you feel content.

想一想颜色对你有什么影响，明亮的颜色会让你高兴吗？阴暗的颜色让你沮丧吗？如果这是你的卧室，你用什么颜色装饰它呢？给这个卧室涂上你感到满意的颜色。

decorate *v.* 装饰